Enjoy Good Health

Enjoy Good Health

A Faith-Based Approach
To Personal Wellness

Rebecca Turner

Copyright © 2020 by Rebecca Turner

ISBN: 978-1-7341033-4-2
Cover design: Virgilio Guardado
Back Cover Photo: Abe Draper
 All rights reserved. No part of this book may be reproduced in any form without written permission from the publisher. Brief passages may be quoted in reviews. WARNING: Unauthorized duplication or downloading is a violation of applicable laws, including U.S. Copyright law. File sharing is allowed only with those companies with which Literary Group has a written agreement.

SARTORIS LITERARY GROUP
Metro-Jackson, Mississippi
www.sartorisliterary.com

To God, thank you for using the weak and foolish things to confound the wise. May your anointing be on this message, not because of me, but in spite of me

CONTENTS

Introduction

Chapter 1
Law versus Grace ... 23

Chapter 2
Define Healthy for Yourself ... 37

Chapter 3
Plan It and Pursue It ... 48

Chapter 4
Grit Meets Grace ... 59

Chapter 5
Your Wellness Thief ... 74

Chapter 6
Give Your Mouth a Detox ...83

Chapter 7
Control Emotional Eating ... 100

Chapter 8
Make Space for Good Health ... 109

Chapter 9
The Cost of Western "Wellness" ... 121

A letter from the author ... 131
Appendix ... 134
About the author ... 137

INTRODUCTION

A David Psalm (The Message)
103 1-2 O my soul, bless God.
From head to toe, I'll bless his holy name!
O my soul, bless God,
don't forget a single blessing!
3-5 He forgives your sins—every one.
He heals your diseases—every one.
He redeems you from hell—saves your life!
He crowns you with love and mercy—a paradise crown.
He wraps you in goodness—beauty eternal.
He renews your youth—you're always young in his presence.

Americans have become fixated on food. Whether it is binge-watching the latest popular cooking contest, or trying the newest fad diet, or declaring yourself a "foodie," it's evident that most of us are obsessed with food. An obsession occurs when one's thoughts or feelings become dominated by food. It's easy to think that someone fixated on food would appear to be overweight, but it also manifests through excessive dieting or anxiety over clean and organic foods. Both ends of the spectrum, including the preoccupation with being a "food snob" without body image issues, exposes a deeper problem: food idolatry.

I have been a registered dietitian for almost a decade. Over the years, I have had a front-row seat to watch the public's interest in food and fitness increase, and the opinions surrounding what we should or should not be eating get as heated and controversial as politics and religion. People have made it their life's work to promote their narrow views of nutrition as optimal, or even magical. Legitimate science that may support a different viewpoint is cast out, overlooked, or countered with false claims. The harassment of others with insults if they disagree on food beliefs has become the new norm, creating contention for the sake of profits. It has been frustrating and heartbreaking to witness.

Now more than ever, the majority stays confused over the continually changing health headlines. Most of you are reluctant about who to believe and are unsure of what to eat. And I don't blame you. Even the nutrition and dietetics profession has found itself picking sides, battling within its inner walls for dominance of opinion. Gone are the days of providing foundational truths to good health and allowing individuals to build a lifestyle around it that makes sense for them. Now it seems every ideology is for itself, cashing in on the lucrative business of health and fitness. All while the consumer, that's you, bears the burden of discouraging results, self-doubt, and unimproved health status.

Simultaneously, an unhealthy obsession with weight, body image, and dietary habits have emerged and taken root in our culture like never before. People are passing judgment on themselves and others based solely on their outward appearance, nutritional principles, and farming practices. Whether you do it outwardly or inwardly, we've all been guilty of bullying ourselves and others for superficial things like weight and food choices. Women, specifically, have abused their mental and physical health to obtain a world view of wellness, while neglecting, or never even pondering what God may have intended for their bodies.

Our pursuit of improving our diet and body image has unleashed a tidal wave of disordered eating behavior like the world has never seen before. Eating disorders are more prevalent than ever. Not everyone who suffers shows signs of being malnourished or underweight. The latest statistics indicate that more than 30 million people in the U.S suffer from an eating disorder. Over 70 percent of those who suffer from eating disorders will avoid treatment due to stigma, misconceptions, lack of education, and overlooked diagnostic opportunity.

Eating disorders have the highest mortality rate of any mental illness, with nearly one person dying every hour as a direct result of an eating disorder. Women over the age of fifty are a fast-growing population for eating disorders at 13 percent. This increase in baby boomers is a reflection of the changing times. Fifty is the new forty, and sixty is the new fifty. Women want to keep going, doing, looking, and feeling great decades longer than other generations. Sadly, this population of women didn't receive adequate education in metabolism after menopause, or how to properly exercise throughout their lifespan, and are reverting to disordered eating patterns to keep up with their ideal lifestyles.

Parents and grandparents of young children should be alarmed to know that the rate of children under twelve who get admitted to a hospital for eating disorders rose 119 percent in less than a decade. Social media and pop culture outlets provide our youth with a 24-hour cycle of body comparison, and one-click to celebrity diet tricks and trends. Without understanding the ramifications of drastic food decisions and feeling pressured to look sexy at a much younger age, our children's mental and physical health is suffering. If you've spent a lifetime of yo-yo dieting, you understand the urgency to help prevent young girls and boys from jumping on the same diet disaster wagon. No parent or caregiver would wish a lifetime of self-loathing on the ones they love the most.

My inbox often is full of messages from parents, teachers, and coaches concerned about their tween or teen who is suffering from aversions to eating and body dysphoria. A sixth-grade teacher reached out to me for help with a student who was so overwhelmed with state testing and keeping up with her competitive sports schedule that she had become terrified to eat at lunch. The thought of putting food to her mouth made her physically nauseous. The stories are endless, but another one from a worried mom that breaks my heart included a teenager who had adopted the mindset, "if you're not starving, you're getting fat." Her daughter would berate herself for eating anything "unclean." These young lives are lucky to have loved ones who spotted the red flags and sought help. But the reality is those precious souls have a long road to recovery, as you well know, food fixation is hard to overcome.

As a nutrition expert, my professional mission has been to help you build balanced meals, find time to exercise and convince you to value taking care of yourself because you are worth it. I still wholeheartedly believe in that mission. Nevertheless, at the core, that well-intended message is flawed, and so is our collective approach to wellness. The majority have lost sight of what was once a movement to eat better, for better health, and they have created an idol out of obtaining the perfect healthy lifestyle. Some of us have allowed our thoughts and feelings around food and self-image to cloud our higher purpose that our Creator intended for us. I believe one of Satan's most significant accomplishments in the Western World is creating the skinny smokescreen, blinding believers, and distracting nonbelievers of their true calling and purpose. You can't be all in for God's vision for your life if you can't take your eyes and mind off a mirror or a scale.

There are a few things in life I know for sure. One, Jesus Christ, is the son of the living God, and I accept His death and resurrection as the only means for sinful humans to be reconciled to God and thereby offered salvation and the promise of eternal life. Two, every believer and nonbeliever on the planet wants to be well. There isn't a single person who woke up this morning just dying to get to Heaven. Not one of you rushed out of bed to check your blood pressure, blood sugar, or scale, giddy to see life-threatening numbers. That would be ludicrous.

While the world provides both the believer and the nonbeliever with an ideal standard of health and happiness, Christians have a secret wellness weapon that doesn't come from pills, powders, food pyramids, or supplements. The difference between believers and nonbelievers is Christians have a guidebook to living a life of purpose, filled to the brim with practical advice for everyday life. It's called the Bible. The problem is that rarely do believers turn to the pages of God's Word for nutrition and fitness advice. I'm trying to change that. Christians should strive to live a life that brings glory to God (1 Corinthians 10:31), and that includes what they choose to eat, why they want to eat it, and how they care for their bodies.

Unfortunately, the Bible doesn't provide us with a detailed diet plan, or a food pyramid, or even instructions on proper exercise. However, food is not excluded entirely from the Bible. As you'll learn, certain foods, feast, and even fasting had biblical significance. In the Old Testament, God performed miracles to supply humans with food. Humans used food to show reverence to God. In the New Testament,

Jesus performed miracles using food, fellowshipped over meals, and even used food as a metaphor for His sacrificial body. These are invaluable life lessons that shouldn't be overlooked but viewed from a broader perspective. These same Biblical principles can be applied today.

While food often appears in the Bible, there is nowhere in the Scripture that says you must have abs, a thigh gap, or completed a marathon to get into heaven. There is not one definitive Bible verse, in the New Testament that says Christians must eat only vegetables, or only non-starchy plants, or forgo food groups or added sugars. Equally so, there is nowhere in the Bible that says you can't pursue a fit physique, achieve athletic greatness, or only eat foods from certain food groups, or grown in a particular manner. That is where the water gets muddy, and people's personal opinions creep in to sway you one way or another.

I believe that Satan has used our food preferences to isolate us from one another and ultimately divide us. Depending on our food ideology of the moment, we become tempted to indulge in food-righteousness, in thinking we're the better person for eating a certain way or avoiding specific ingredients. As believers, our gospel doesn't leave room for self-made righteousness. Before God, apart from Christ, "None is righteous, no, not one" (Romans 3:10). Jesus sacrificed His life to atone for our sins so that we wouldn't have to work for our righteousness. It's a gift from God, not based on the merits of our behavior, including our food choices or body weight. That doesn't make our diet meaningless, but it should make believers, of all people, humble about what we and everyone else chooses to eat.

My purpose with this book is to shift your focus to eat with Jesus in mind and not for the world's standards. To understand foundational principles within God's Word that apply to all areas of life, but can and will help you mend your relationship with food. At this point in my professional career, I'm less worried about what you are eating, and much more concerned with why you are eating it. It is time to take food and self-image off the idol pedestal and put it back where God intends it. I'm here to challenge your lust for a particular self-image and help you free yourself of those strongholds in the form of rigid food rules and decades of worldly doctrine stealing precious time away from your true calling and purpose. Or, merely robbing you of joy.

If you are interested in my professional nutrition ideology, you can pick up my book, *Mind Over Fork*. In that book, I provide a personal recall of my journey to self-awareness and the tools that helped me build a positive relationship with food, providing practical eating strategies backed by time-tested science. Even though I have a bachelor's and a master's degree in nutrition and dietetics, I, too, struggle to break free from the grip of the world's view of wellness. I know what it is like to not like the skin you're in, to measure your self-worth by the number on the scale, and to spend more time counting calories than time in prayer. I've been down the road of trying to look and eat perfect, and it landed me further and further away from God and genuine joy.

You have heard that your bodies are temples of the Holy Spirit, and you should honor God with your bodies (1 Corinthians 6:16). It is often used in the Christian wellness arena to demonstrate that how we care for bodies matters to God. This is true, but traditionally this verse can leave us with more guilt and shame than encouragement when we can't live up to perfect temple keepers. It wasn't until after having both of my girls that God showed me how to perceive this revelation differently. There have been two times in my life when I can say my relationship with food was at its healthiest, meaning, I ate for the sole purpose of nourishing my body. Both of those times were when I was pregnant with my girls. I took the responsibility of being pregnant seriously and intentionally didn't let my disordered eating habits affect the health and wellbeing of my growing baby. My unborn child meant more to me than my desire to manipulate food for an outward appearance gain.

Finally, one day it just clicked when studying 1 Corinthians 6:16, and I recognized that being the vessel for the Holy Spirit is just as significant as being pregnant with an unborn child. What I fed my body, mind, and spirit would ultimately determine how strong and healthy the Holy Spirit would be in me. I couldn't fully work in tandem with the Holy Spirit while neglecting its vessel, my body. My body has a higher purpose than to be the doormat to my worldly insecurities. I would never treat God the way I treated my body for years. Yet ironically, that is what I was doing without grasping it. Being disrespectful to your body by the way you think about it, talk about it, feed it, or mistreat it, is a direct action to the Holy Spirit living on the inside. Understanding 1 Corinthians 6:19 was a game-changing moment for me and my relationship with my physical form. It's not about me, and it never will be again.

As believers, you and I are called to live a life for Jesus, and it is time Christians start eating for Him too.

This book is inspired by Scripture, the stories, people, and parables throughout the pages, along with my reflections. I'd encourage you to avoid simply reading over the verses mentioned in this book, but pause and take time to look them up in your Bible. Throughout, you will find opportunities to go deeper into your thoughts and feelings with journaling style questions labeled "explore." Avoid the urge to skip over these. Start a journal to allow God to use these questions as a catalyst for uncovering your truth. Integrate the "explore" exercises and the provided Bible verses into your daily prayer life and devotional time. Make this book more than another book to read. The upcoming pages should be a personal excavation to understand your relationship with food and self-image better.

The New International Version (NIV) of the Bible is the primary source of verses. Feel free to explore the various versions surrounding each Scripture. Take the lead to read the entire chapter of a verse shared. Often, it is the verses around a critical verse that shine a light on the moral of the story. The Bible is similar to a complicated recipe when you skip ingredients or skim through the instructions you don't always get the best-tasting meal. While you may learn something Biblical along the way, my prayer is that you discover more about yourself.

At the beginning of the introduction, you read Psalm 103 1-5 from The Message. Other versions of this Psalm drive home the same idea, but this one spoke to me. In my life, it is a prime example of meditating on God's promises, without paying attention to God's request. Like many, I highlighted and focused on verses 3-5 of Psalm 103.

Who doesn't want their sins forgiven, diseases healed, and be crowned with love and mercy? And let's face it, most of our "wellness" desires are really in vain—a longing for youth! Isn't that what you want, after all? Fewer wrinkles, a tight tushy, and to be able to run, jump, and play at any decade? That's youth. The desire to be youthful and healthy is as universal as the desire for shelter, plenty of food, to feel safe and to have opportunities to thrive. No one wishes against good health. It's unnatural. You and I hold tight to God's promises, but fail to focus on the first two verses, which are the prerequisites to wellbeing. We agree we all want to be well, but we might not all realize we can't get to wellness without worship.

In Psalm 103, David understands that true worship is something deeply inward, of the soul. It's not just bumper stickers, singing praise songs, church attendance, or checking off a daily devotional or liking Bible verses online. True worship is an inward lifestyle that springs from your soul. In The Message version, David called for everything from his head to his toe, to give honor and praise to God for every single blessing. That is going all in! What a call to action for believers! When you finally take inventory of every unique merit of favor God has bestowed on you, the remembrance alone will provide you all the reasons to stay in contestant praise.

I don't want you to miss the fundamental truth before moving on to the rest of the book. Once the scale tips to more time spent in praise and worship than obsessing over food and your figure, you'll start to see a wellness transformation from the inside out. I can't promise you that worshiping God is the weight loss tool you've been praying for, or that you don't need to put in some effort in changing your lifestyle to improve your health. Still, I can guarantee you that you will never reach true wellness, no matter your weight or athletic achievements, without worship. When your priorities are in place, God will move on your behalf, and whether the pounds fall off or you experience a peace that passes understanding with you accepting your thighs, you'll know it's a God thing, and He'll receive the honor and glory.

As a friendly reminder, Christians are called to live a life for Jesus. Now it is time to explore how to eat for him, too.

A Word of Caution

Those diagnosed with an eating disorder, such as anorexia nervosa, bulimia nervosa, or binge eating, will not get sufficient help from the suggestions presented in this book. You should connect with your primary care provider or reach out to an outpatient clinic that specializes in disorder eating evaluation and counseling.

According to the American Academy of Family Physicians, you should ask yourself the following questions:

1. Are you underweight, but tell others you are overweight even when they say you are skinny?
2. After eating food, do you ever try to get rid of the food by making yourself vomit or by taking laxatives?
3. Do you use food to control your emotions to the extremes, and has it caused you to gain excessive weight and experience even more sadness over gaining weight?
4. Do you spend a lot of time worrying about how you look? Does this excessive worry keep you from social activities, or completing your work?

5. Have you stopped having periods even though you have not entered menopause?
6. Have you noticed find hair growing on your body?

Answering yes to any of the above questions indicates you could benefit from a consultation with a trained psychologist or physician. Getting proper treatment for mental health disorders such as anxiety or depression will help you best.

You can also visit the National Eating Disorders Association (NEDA) website for a more detailed online survey for those ages 13 and up to determine if it's time to seek professional help. The NEDA Helpline is available Monday-Thursday from 9 AM to 9 PM ET, and Friday from 9 AM to 5 PM ET. Contact the Helpline for support, resources, and treatment options for yourself or a loved one. (800) 931-2237.

Enjoy Good Health

Chapter 1
Law vs Grace

"Under the law, even the best fail.
Under grace, even the worst can be saved"—Joseph Prince

Can you remember the anticipation for your sixteenth birthday? Finally, freedom is yours with the license to drive. To a young adult, the potential that comes with your first set of car keys is endless. I remember daydreaming of getting to roll down the windows, feel the wind in my hair, turn my music up loud, and head off into an open road full of adventure. Finally, the day came for my dad to hand over the keys to a 99' Sunfire with tinted windows and a sunroof. Before I could burst at the seams with excitement and pull out of the driveway, headed to a friend's house, reality sunk in. Dad derailed the transferring of ownership, to lay down some hard ground rules around driving.

"I will not tolerate a speeding ticket in this house," dad said with a stern face. He continued, "Speeding tickets are easy to avoid. You don't speed!"

Like all parents, my dad understood the dangers of the road and only wanted what was best for my safety. Speeding and breaking the rules of the road would put me in danger, cause potential harm to myself and others. There was nothing inherently wrong with his ground rules, but at the tender age of sixteen, I didn't hear the concern in his voice, only the demand to be perfect. My interpretation of his rules went like this, "It's easy not to get a speeding ticket. Just drive perfect." Upholding a blemish-free driving record morphed into decades of being trapped in the prison of perfectionism.

The Israelites must have felt intense pressure and anxiety when they sought to follow God in the Old Testament. Back then, they were expected to walk correctly in all the ways that God had commanded.

> So be careful to do what the Lord your God has commanded you; do not turn aside to the right or to the left. Walk in obedience to all that the Lord your God has commanded you, so that you may live and prosper and prolong your days in the land that you will possess. Deuteronomy 5:32-33 (NIV)

Imagine what it must have been like for the Israelites to see the Ten Commandments for the very first time. I assume it would be similar to my anxiety surrounding my dad's driving rules, times a thousand. Messing up one of God's rules isn't just getting grounded from your driving privileges, but potentially missing out on Heaven!

Explore: Do you feel anxious thinking about keeping God's standards? Do you struggle with a false sense of security that you might gain a reward if you act correctly? What about if you eat ideally?

God wanted His people to enjoy His blessings, so He provided a standard for how they should live. He was direct in communicating His will; He gave them the law, which was a blueprint for how He wanted us to live. Deuteronomy 5:32

reminds us to be careful to do what the Lord your God has commanded you.

Born again, Christians are aware of the Lord's instructions. Chances are you read your Bible, do devotionals, engage in the pastor's teachings, and engage in life groups within your home church. You check off all the "good" Christian boxes for your daily living. Even with all your knowledge and confessed faith, you find yourself slipping, unable to do it all. The Ten Commandments are easy to keep, just not easy to maintain all ten in one day. Bottom line, even with the best intentions, you're unable to live up to God's holy standard. And that is okay. You're certainly not alone.

> *For all who rely on the works of the law are under a curse, as it is written: "Cursed is everyone who does not continue to do everything written in the Book of the Law." Clearly no one who relies on the law is justified before God, because "the righteous will live by faith." The law is not based on faith; on the contrary, it says, "The person who does these things will live by them." Galatians 3:10-12 (NIV)*

Let's go back to the collective experience of getting your driver's license. For the majority of adults, driving is a universal privilege that comes with age. However, there are stipulations to maintaining the license to drive, such as following traffic laws, put in place for public safety. Whether you and I agree with the speed limit or groan at a slow traffic light, we are required to uphold the law, or we stand to lose our privilege to drive. And even if you have a perfect driving record, you can't honestly say you've never broken a driving rule. If you've driven long enough, you have at least once operated with a heavy foot, accidentally rolled through a stop sign, or failed to use your blinker.

It didn't take long after getting behind the wheel of a shiny new car to collect my first ding, and eventually a road violation. Fear, shame, and guilt built up inside, knowing I would have to face my dad with a failure of not keeping the law of the road perfect. I can remember scrounging around, trying to figure out how to fix it before taking it to him. Hoping that my willingness to take ownership would curve any frustrations he might have against me. The accident happened in a split second, but the looming dread felt like it lasted a lifetime. Although there were consequences to breaking the rules, there was also grace from my dad. Much to my surprise, he was more concerned with my safety than my driving record and used it as a teachable moment for the future. I will never forget the mercy he showed over something as trivial as a minor car mishap.

Explore: Have you ever received grace from someone of authority, friend, or family member? How did you feel before receiving the olive branch? What did it mean to you to be offered forgiveness, regardless of the incident?

Driving laws are ubiquitous to all of us who hold a valid driver's license. The same goes for Christians and the Ten Commandments. While all believers should do their best to uphold God's moral law daily, chances are you and I are going to blunder more than once from sunup to sundown. Typically, individuals struggle with a few cardinal sins more than others.

Like driving, for example. You may have a lead foot, where I hardly ever speed, but I sometimes find it hard to come to a complete stop on a deserted country road. It's easy to become fixated on our stifling sins and get wrapped up in our inability to extinguish them. You can feel just as guilt-stricken over daily struggles with the small things as you do when there is an unforeseen and often accidental big slip. The Apostle Paul had the same battle with stubborn sins as we do today. He explains the paradox perfectly in the seventh chapter of Romans.

> *I do not understand what I do. For what I want to do I do not do, but what I hate I do. And if I do what I do not want to do, I agree that the law is good. As it is, it is no longer I myself who do it, but it is sin living in me. For I know that good itself does not dwell in me, that is, in my sinful nature. For I have the desire to do what is good, but I cannot carry it out. For I do not do the good I want to do, but the evil I do not want to do—this I keep on doing. Now if I do what I do not want to do, it is no longer I who do it, but it is sin living in me that does it. Romans 7:15-20 (NIV)*

Explore: Be open and honest with yourself about those stifling sins. What areas of your life do you wish you could get a better hold? When it comes to your food and fitness routines, what are the most challenging habits you have to end or jumpstart?

News flash, God, isn't shocked when you and I are unable to walk the straight and narrow. The law was created in the Old Testament to provide a moral standard. Thank you, Jesus, that Christians today are living after His death and resurrection. Today, Christ-followers reap the reward of the only One that was capable of living in perfect obedience.

> *So the law was our guardian until Christ came that we might be justified by faith. Now that this faith has come, we are no longer under a guardian. Galatians 3: 24-25 (NIV)*

You might think that if it is impossible to live up to God's perfect standard, why try? Well, if everyone didn't "try" to follow the rules of the road, there would be a lot more casualties due to carefree driving. Followers of Christ should strive to uphold the Old Testament commandments, allowing it to convict us, not condemn us. Christians are to obey out of a heart for Christ and a desire to please Him, not because *you* will get struck by lightning if they mess up.

By now, you might be wondering where the healthy living mentality comes into this rundown of law versus grace. I'm glad you asked. You must understand the foundation of how Christians are supposed to approach the ideology of doing and being perfect for achieving salvation or God's love. I hope you now have a renewed sense that by design, you are unable to uphold God's law perfectly. In essence, God knew you needed a savior from the rigid rules.

If, by design, you are unable to upload God's law correctly, why do you expect or ever expected, you would be able to adhere to strict food rules? The same imperfect flesh that slips on the Ten Commandments will undoubtedly fail you with silly eating rules. Finding freedom to live your healthiest life means you learn to approach eating with the same faith and grace that comes with living your best Christ-like life. You look to time-tested nutrition principles to guide your food choices, not dictate them. You learn to offer yourself grace, instead of condemnation over food choices and have faith that perfection isn't required to be in good health.

Explore: Spend time writing down any fad diets, food trends, or diet ideologies that have become nutrition "law" for you. Explore the good the bad and the ugly of your diet decisions of the past. Look back over those notes. Ask yourself when you were unable to uphold these general food rules, how did you feel about yourself?

Food Rules in Biblical Law

Everyone needs to eat, including the people in the Bible. Historical societies and religions of all kinds practiced or actively practiced some form of dietary restriction for a vast array of reasons. Biblical law is no different. Within the Old Testament, there are several significant periods where there are various forms of food rules, and then there is food freedom found in the New Testament.

Whether there are or are not food rules in the Bible is not what is up for debate. However, for the last two thousand years, people have pondered why the Old Testament was riddled with such a complex system of food guidelines. God gave His people comprehensive regulations surrounding what, how, and when they are to consume certain foods, but the Bible fails to offer any detailed explanation underlying the purpose. Since I am a registered dietitian and not a Biblical scholar, I'll leave those intense debates up to someone else. What I do find noteworthy was the context around the different periods of food rules and, most importantly, what the New Testament brings to believers and their food choices.

In the beginning, God created Heaven and Earth, and as early as Genesis, the Bible tells that people should eat appropriate foods. Before God has even completed creation, He provides the first sentiment on what He considers suitable for consumption. Stating He gives us every seed-bearing plant on the face of the whole earth and every tree that has fruit with seeds in it. Food was meant not only to nourish the body but also for pleasure. God created man with taste buds to relish in the sweetness of an apple, or tanginess of a plum. By design, humans pause to eat throughout the day, with hunger being a cue and reminder of our dependence on God to nourish and sustain our bodies with food.

> *Then God said, "I give you every seed-bearing plant on the face of the whole earth and every tree that has fruit with seed in it. They will be yours for food. And to all the beasts of the earth and all the birds in the sky and all the creatures that move along the ground—everything that has the breath of life in it—I give every green plant for food." And it was so. Genesis 1: 29-30 (NIV)*

Humans and animals started with a vegan or plant-only diet. These rules were all before the fall of humanity. The one food rule broken known throughout the ages, was Adam and Eve defying God and eating from the tree of knowledge of good and evil. Breaking this command results in their expulsion from the Garden of Eden and ultimately sends humanity down a very different historical path. The next time God points out the human diet is in Leviticus, specifically in chapter 11, after the great flood destroyed the world. There you see the first Biblical reference to humans expanding their menu to include meat.

> *The Lord said to Moses and Aaron, "Say to the Israelites: 'Of all the animals that live on land, these are the ones you may eat: Leviticus 11: 1-2 (NIV)*

However, further reading into Leviticus will showcase a whole host of food instructions that limit the people who survived the flood to choosing only certain kinds of animals, sea life, and birds. Read for yourself the laundry list of regulations. Notably, all humanity is firmly instructed never to eat flesh with life still in it, meaning its blood. Interestingly, God is good at giving them profound principals to eat by, but no real reason why other than He said so. That indeed is proof enough to do our best to follow His Almighty command. But, imagine being the home-cook and trying to come up with a weekly menu that met all of God's guidelines, plus meals your family would eat. In today's home kitchens, you'd have home cooks having meltdowns left and right.

If you thought that Noah and his family had hard to follow rules around food, wait till you get a taste of the people of Israel's daily requirements. They are more intense than the previous dietary guidelines. You start to see God's people instructed on which animals may be eaten down to the specific parts that are allowed for consumption. There are instructions on how to prepare animals for consumption on using animals for sacrificial offerings to the Lord. Spend time in Leviticus and Deuteronomy to see all the food rules, but know that this is where a lot of the debate and speculation by Biblical scholars is focused still today. As if they will ever really uncover what God's mindset was behind giving such a detailed to-eat and not-to-eat list.

Again, my purpose with this book is not to make you Biblical scholars on food rules of the past. I do hope I have sparked interest in you to go and read those chapters with a new purpose and put yourself in the shoes of those early Jews before Christ (BC). My main intention is to set the stage with what was going on BC and open your eyes and hearts to the profound changes Jesus brought to believers' everyday life after His death and resurrection (AD). I realize that different denominations have different definitions of BC and AD—for some, AD comes from the Latin, *anno Domini,* which translates to "the year of the Lord," while others feel AD stands for "After Deliverance," thus presenting different mathematical calculations—so I will use BC and AD according to how I have been taught and allow you to do your own math according to how you have been taught. Welcome to the New Testament, where home cooks are free to put healthy meals on the table without first dissecting a carcass.

Even after Christ had died and resurrected, setting Christians free from the law and offering up grace, there were still false teachers who told believers to abstain from certain foods to be more Godly. In their defense, their family's culinary traditions were hardwired with certain foods that were considered good, or bad, or Biblical and safe or unclean.

Remember, if they weren't two thousand years removed from BC, chances are they had family members who were alive before Christ and the reverent fear to follow the rules was sewn into the fabric of society.

Explore: It may not be to the degree as the BC Jews, but does your family have unwritten food rules that have been passed down from generation to generation? You could have been taught to cook with lard, save your bacon grease, sustain from pork, or only eat fish on Friday during Lent. These aren't always negative unwritten rules; some can be very spiritual. Spend time pondering what you were raised to believe about food.

> *For everything God created is good, and nothing is to be rejected if it is received with thanksgiving, because it is consecrated by the word of God and prayer. 1 Timothy 4: 4-5 (NIV)*

The Apostle Paul directly speaks to these false, fear-based teachings suggesting that everything God created is good, and nothing is to be rejected if it is received with thanksgiving, because the word of God and prayer consecrates it. You will spend some time exploring the spiritual significance of gratitude in an upcoming chapter, but for now, fully know that when Jesus died, so did the dietary laws of the Old Testament.

You should rejoice and realize that Christians no longer have to label foods "good" or "bad" or in Biblical terms "clean" or "unclean." Paul recognized that by design, believers want to "do good" to gain the upper hand with God. And he further touches on the hard-to-die food theories in his instructions to the church at Corinth, letting members know that your food choices no longer bring you nearer to God. You are no more or less a Christian based on what you eat. Can I get an Amen!

> *But food does not bring us near to God; we are no worse if we do not eat, and no better if we do. 1 Corinthians 8:8 (NIV)*

Romans 6:18 proclaims that Christians have been set free from sin. As God's children, we are allowed and should experience the glorious freedom and liberty Jesus died to give us—freedom to enjoy all that God has given to us through His Son. That includes the freedom to love our bodies and enjoy nourishing foods of all kinds. You don't get a free ticket to the buffet line or become a couch potato. We will address that later, but for now, start to enjoy your freedom from body expectations and food law.

I pray you are starting to see the potential to change the perspective of your health and wellness journey to one that takes you deep into your faith. Feeling guilty and condemned all the time over food and your pants size is not freedom. Being in mental and emotional turmoil is not freedom. Grace is the power of the Holy Spirit in our lives, enabling us to whatever God instructs us to do. That includes managing our health and our weight. When you submit to the Holy Spirit's promptings and trust that is God guiding you, you will have the power to drive past a drive-thru, get up early for your workout, ditch your scale, walk past the doughnuts, break free from body dysmorphia and experience newness of life. Thank God, we can break out the skinny trap and start enjoying our blood-bought freedom.

Fasting in the Bible

Fasting is a time-honored spiritual tradition. Almost every religion has some fasting ritual. Jesus, Plato, Socrates, and Gandhi did it. Not to mention, there is Lent, Ramadan, Yom Kippur, and other traditions. A religious fast has deeper intentions than the attempt to fit into a pair of jeans. You must separate spiritual gains from ancient holy fasts from labeling it science or health-promoting. The Daniel Fast is often touted as a sustainable lifestyle, yet that was not its intention in the Bible. Even the Daniel Fast served a higher purpose and was endured for a limited time.

> *"When you fast, do not look somber as the hypocrites do, for they disfigure their faces to show others they are fasting. Truly I tell you, they have received their reward in full. But when you fast, put oil on your head and wash your face, so that it will not be obvious to others that you are fasting, but only to your Father, who is unseen; and your Father, who sees what is done in secret, will reward you. Matthew 6: 16-18*

In the Bible, you will find references to fasting in both the Old and the New Testaments. However, in the New Testament, Jesus never gives direct instructions on how and when to fast, just that it is part of godly living. Matthew 6: 16-18 shows Jesus teaching His disciples basic principles of following Him, and at the foundation of giving, prayer, and fasting, it should always be done for the right reasons with the right mindset. Jesus states, "when you fast," not "if you fast." You can interpret that fasting of some kind has its place as a follower of Christ.

The world glamorizes eating patterns like intermittent fasting and detox as a way to recharge or renew your body. The Bible never glamorizes fasting. Biblical characters, including Jesus, entered a fast seeking a deeper connection with God. Throughout the Bible, fasting was used to prepare for ministry, seek God's wisdom, show grief, obtain deliverance or protection, to repent, gain victory, or to further worship God. Christians should incorporate fasting into their relationship with Christ, but that doesn't have to be in the form of food rules, and should always be done with sincere intentions. The bottom line: fasting, was never intended as a practical or sustainable weight loss tool.

Our prayer: *Lord, I confess I need your grace and guidance in healing my relationship with food. Grant me the grace that draws me into your will for my health and may I love myself as you have loved me. Lord, I want the health and life that you've planned for me. I can't be that without surrender of food laws, self-defeating mindsets, and unhealthy habits. Show me what it means for me to be surrendered and empower me to obey your promptings for better health at all cost. Amen.*

Chapter 2
Define Healthy for Yourself

2-3 And then God answered: "Write this.
   Write what you see.
Write it out in big block letters
   so that it can be read on the run.
This vision-message is a witness
   pointing to what's coming.
It aches for the coming—it can hardly wait!
   And it doesn't lie.
If it seems slow in coming, wait.
   It's on its way. It will come right on time.
Habakkuk 2:2-3 The Message (MSG)

    Undoubtedly, Christians should feel relieved that Jesus came and not only atoned for our sins but also relieved us of the law, including those pesky and complicated food regulations. However, fast forward two thousand years and believers today, especially those living in the West, would benefit from a better directive on how to eat for good health. Imagine what the twelve disciples, who walked the earth with Jesus, would think about the decisions today's Christians face while in the grocery store. The selection of food alone would overwhelm them, and the reality of massive food waste with starving people across the ocean would probably break their hearts.

    Once again, the Bible does not explicitly describe what

good health for believers looks like in menu form. What is in the Bible are plenty of parables, proverbs, and Scriptures that give insight into how individuals should go about creating a healthy vision for their life. Many of you are lost and wandering through life without a wellness plan, not fully understanding what you want out of your health. Even the dictionary does a poor job helping us figure out what healthy living means. Webster Dictionary defines "healthy" as being free from disease or pain. That is a good start, but that leaves so much to the imagination.

Explore: Before moving forward, take time to jot down what words or ideas come to mind when you meditate on the word healthy. Also, add those who have influenced your ideology around good health. It could be doctors, friends, media, celebrities, etc. There are no right or wrong answers, just your thoughts on paper.

Without being able to see your list, I would dare to assume that the health and wellness industry has influenced some of your answers. With it being a multi-billion dollar industry, product companies, gym owners, magazine editors, and social media influencers have made an abundant living complicating wellness for the sake of profits. The formal definition of healthy leaves a wide gap between being free from chronic disease and suffering from pain, to what is on magazine covers, or your social media feed. Confusing and conflicting nutrition and fitness information keep consumers, like you, spending money on the latest fad. Industry pockets become lined with cash, while the general public receives little to zero real health gains.

ENJOY GOOD HEALTH

As your registered dietitian and friend, I can't tell you exactly what good health will look like for you and your family. However, I do honestly pray that you enjoy good health, and all may go well with your soul. The idea of enjoying good health comes from 3 John 1:2. The third book of John was a letter to Gaius, a member of the church. And although we don't know the author of this book for sure, most scholars believe it was John.

> *Dear friend, I pray that you may enjoy good health and that all may go well with you, even as your soul is getting along well. 3 John 1:2 (NIV)*

Depending on the version of the verse you read, you'll see slightly different text. It is important to note and clarify that back in John's time, verbs, like prosper and be in health, belonged to the everyday language of letter writing, much like our everyday uses of sincerely, or have a great day. At no time did John imply that this phrase meant that Christ's followers would have perpetual wealth or good health. Nor do I want to suggest that only Godly people enjoy good health and that you can get better health by being a better Christian. There are many lifestyle habits a Christian can observe that may improve their overall health and wellbeing. But you are not being punished by God if you develop a chronic disease, struggle to maintain an ideal weight, or find yourself with a devastating health report.

As one friend encourages another, which is what John is doing, my heart's desire is for you to enjoy good health brought about by honoring God in your choices and stewarding the body He has given you. And sometimes that means doing our humanly best within less than ideal situations. You can still enjoy good health at any stage of life, age, size, or health status. It is up to you, your life choices, and your mindset to find fulfillment in what today's health brings. If you live long enough, good health will take on a variety of phases. Let me explain further what I desire for you in terms of enjoyment.

What you enjoy and what you think you have to achieve to accomplish good health are often quite different. The same paradox applies to what you need to weigh to be in good health versus what you want to weigh. Medically speaking, for those clinically diagnosed as overweight or obese, it often only takes a 10 percent loss of body weight to dramatically improve your blood pressure and fasting blood sugar, or lower your risk of certain cancers. Research published in the *Journal of the National Cancer Institute*, suggests women over the age of 50 who lose as little as 4 lbs—and keep it off—may lower their risk of developing breast cancer.

Your ideal weight that you desire to reach is typically much lower, for vanity reasons, not for health outcomes. While there is no shame in wanting to push your physical exterior to the limits, you must remember that there is always a price to pay for just five more pounds lost. Typically, once you've hit a number that makes you medically healthy, it's your joy that gets lost trying to chase the world's standard of skinny. You are more likely to backslide and lose all the healthy habits you created by infinitely trying to improve your weight or figure. At some point, your body must be enough for you.

For some getting to a state of mind and body that one can enjoy good health might require weight gain. Weight gain due to a release of ridged food rules and rituals will happen naturally and level off as you become more comfortable with learning your hunger cues. Trusting yourself to know when you're full enough is a tough concept for many of us to comprehend. The wellness industry is positioned to glorify weight loss and avoid weight gain at all costs. But sometimes the cost of losing weight or living in a smaller body isn't worth the mental and spiritual anguish. I know this from personal experience. I spent most of my twenties chasing a smaller body size, and it had nothing to do with overall health. I forfeited so much good food, and opportunities to better enjoy the moment, by obsessing on eating the perfect macronutrient balance and staying within the caloric boundaries I had set for myself. I'm proud to say I am twenty pounds heavier and have never felt healthier or been happier with my relationship with food.

You can start to create a definition for enjoying good health that lines up with your individual preferences and needs. Enjoy is defined as taking pleasure in or satisfaction in something. When putting adequate health and enjoyment together, you find that it means whatever you find joy and happiness in that keeps you free of chronic illness or pain. Now you have more ammo to help better define your definition of healthy. Don't look to the right or left when determining "good health." Instead ask yourself straight forward questions about what you want out of your health.

Explore: Take out a sheet of paper and first right down every diet that you have ever attempted, whether it was low-carb, low-fat, or specific calorie count, or prescribed to you by a health care provider such as diabetic-friendly, heart-healthy.

Now, on that same sheet draw two columns and label one pro and the other con. Go through each diet you've ever attempted, and without any judgment, ask yourself what you enjoyed about that diet and what you disliked. Assessing past dieting attempts is a helpful tool to start to see patterns of behavior. Be mindful of what thoughts and feelings keep popping up for the pros and the cons. Use this to assist you when you start to define healthy living for yourself.

You may wonder why you should put so much effort into organizing your thoughts, feelings, and ideas about living a healthy life on paper. The Bible tells us that people with a plan and vision were more likely to succeed. It is often referred to as a "health and wellness journey" because there is some ending that one desires. Think about it. You will never go to an airport, call on an Uber, or wait at the bus stop without having planned out where to end up. In essence, you can travel anywhere you want to as long as you know where that is, and you can afford to get there.

Your ideal healthy life may include getting off medications, making physical activity a daily priority, growing a garden, drinking more water, or learning how to prepare nourishing meals. For others, it could be bending themselves into a pretzel with advanced yoga, lifting heavy weights, running fast and far, or climbing tall mountains. You might even see yourself finishing a 5K, half or full marathon, riding a bike to work, or learning to roller skate. Don't discount the mediocre, middle of the road kind of good health. You don't have to conquer the food and fitness world to be healthy. It's okay just to want to manage or prevent chronic disease and be able to do daily activities. Your vision can also change as you start to manifest it into reality, taking it to the next level, or not, it is up to you. What is not up for debate is whether or not you create a vision for what a healthy life looks like for you and you only. Wandering without a map gets you lost.

There are two rules for creating a healthy vision for your life. First, you're not allowed to use numbers (i.e., weight or pants size) that are not associated with biological markers (i.e., blood pressure, blood sugar, cholesterol) as part of your vision. Remember, there is not one place in the Bible that says, "thou shalt be a size 4 to get into the pearly gates." Second, you must explore your motivation behind your vision. Motivation is the act or process of giving yourself a reason for something. It is the force or influence that causes you to take or refute action. The Bible talks a great deal about motivation, and Christians are supposed to be motivated by what pleases God in all we do. That includes what you eat, drink, and how you move.

> *So whether you eat or drink or whatever you eat or drink or whatever you do, do it all for the glory of God. 1 Corinthians 10:31 (NIV)*

To get the full depth of 1 Corinthians 10:31, read the surrounding text, including verses 23-33. You will find Paul trying to ease the anxiety of the Corinthian Christians who are still very familiar with food laws and regulations before Christ (BC). In the last chapter, I had you ponder the food rules that have dictated your food choices. Some may have included, but were not limited too, restricting carbs, removing dietary fats, not eating past a specific time, or that fruit is unhealthy because of sugar. You recognize how hard it is to break the cycle of these self-inflicted food laws that you have taught yourself over the years. Think how hard it would be to let these dietary ideologies go if you thought they came from God!

The Apostle Paul had a big task on his hands to help Christians take a big deep breath and trust the freedom found in being a believer after Jesus's death and resurrection (AD). Even freedom in their diet! As you read through 1 Corinthians 10, you find Paul sharing that post-resurrection, everything is technically permissible, but don't go crazy because not everything is beneficial. It is true, there is no more law, and God is not in the role of decision making for you in life, much less at the dinner table. However, just because you now have free will to choose for yourself what to eat, you must be mindful of how those choices are affecting your health. Paul hammers home in verse 30 that if he took part in a meal with thankfulness, a heart full of gratitude and joy, why would he be denounced or condemned for it? Not only by God but by another sitting at the table. Meaning you can enjoy your steak with a vegan or take satisfaction in your croissant while dining with a low-carb lover.

Explore: Ask yourself the same questions about how you treat yourself after enjoying a dessert or French fries. If you approached the meal with true thanksgiving and gratitude, why do you leave the meal with guilt, shame, or condemnation? That is not from God. Also, ponder how you change the way you dine when you are around certain people. Are you influenced by their choices or eat differently out of fear of judgment?

There is a chance that hearing that "anything goes" creates more confusion for you. Don't allow doubt to creep in.

ENJOY GOOD HEALTH

Because of God's immense grace, believers no longer have to scrutinize every action or food decision to see if it is lawful. But Paul's point in 1 Corinthians is that he doesn't want Christians to "get by" with life. While Paul is utilizing the food choices as a teaching tool to experience other biblical implications that go well beyond the plate, don't miss the simplicity of the message that can apply to your everyday life. You want to strive still to live well and utilize a common-sense approach to the basics. The Message version of 1 Corinthians 10: 31-33 sums up what I'm trying to relay to you best.

> *31-33 So eat your meals heartily, not worrying about what others say about you—you're eating to God's glory, after all, not to please them. As a matter of fact, do everything that way, heartily and freely to God's glory. At the same time, don't be callous in your exercise of freedom, thoughtlessly stepping on the toes of those who aren't as free as you are. I try my best to be considerate of everyone's feelings in all these matters; I hope you will be, too. The Message*

Ultimately, your motives will determine your success. And while you may reach your desired number on the scale, you can't call it a success if you're living in bondage on the inside. The truth is only you and God know what is motivating your healthy vision. Deep down, you know whether or not your desire to diet or exercise is encouraged by vanity, envy, fear, shame, or to be the best steward of God's vessel. There is nothing biblically wrong with wanting to get back into your pre-baby jeans or setting the bar high for your nutritional standards. You run into spiritual concern if you lose focus or have an inability to enjoy the good health you have today.

Keep this question visible in your Bible or on your refrigerator to check in with your motives often: Do you spend more time worrying about your weight than you do in the worship of your Creator?

Chances are if you have been chasing the same vision or ideas for decades and continue to fall off the wagon, then your motivation was never rooted in a firm foundation. Creating the right image for yourself will take more than 15 minutes if you have spent the last fifteen years being conditioned by the world to view health in only one capacity: thin and attractive. Don't overlook the power of a well-prayed-about, well-thought-through healthy vision for your life. Don't be afraid to go rogue with your ideas and break free from past ideologies. Pray and ask God to give you His vision for your health, your energy, and your body. Seek His will for what a healthy image looks like for you.

Explore: Go back to the words and phrases you jotted down that represent healthy living for you. Circle the ones that bring you joy and cross out the ones that cause you anxiety. To further explore your definition of healthy, complete the healthy vision worksheet found in the appendix. Keep in mind that your vision can be a living document in which goals may change depending on the stage of life you're experiencing. It's not the Ten Commandments, but you should have an idea of what food boundaries and health aspirations work for you.

Circle back to the beginning of this chapter at the verse Habakkuk: 2: 2-3 and put it to use with your newly found healthy vision. Once you have a better idea of what wellness looks like for you, it is essential to put that vision where you can see it often. Your brain is trained to go back to what is most familiar. By keeping this new vision in front of you, you help re-train your mind and bring it to life. These verses remind us of the importance of being on the watch for impatience when our visions don't come to fruition as fast as we'd prefer. Once you go to God requesting an idea for good health, you must observe the answers God gives by his Word, His Spirit, and then do your part. You do your part by coming up with a plan of action.

Our prayer - *Lord, I don't want anything to come between my heart and your vision for my health. If it means I give up the world's standards for wellness, so be it. Your vision is more powerful, fruitful, and obtainable than my broken view of healthy. Help me to surrender my tainted ideology of good health and beauty and trust in your vision for me. Amen.*

Chapter 3
Plan it and Pursue it

If you forfeit the process, you forfeit the promise—Steffany Gretzinger

Hopefully, you spent time creating a healthy vision for yourself. If not, don't read another line into this chapter until you complete that task. Again, it is good to remind yourself that your vision should be a living perspective that will change as your life and goals do. God wrote the Ten Commandments in stone; your vision for your life is allowed to be fluid, but not fleeting. The concept is only your starting point. It is a visual idea of how your destination will look. When planning your ideal vacation, you ultimately come to a conclusion of where you want to travel. Next, you have to put into motion a plan that will get you to that chosen destination. A vision, no matter how well thought out, doesn't manifest itself by hanging on a wall or being written in a journal. You've got to walk it out, and you can't do that without a little planning on the forefront and a whole lot of action.

Some of the Bible's most notable stories and characters are prime examples of God providing humans with a plan that would change the course of history. As you'll see through a few remarkable biblical stories, God didn't do the work for them. Through prayer, trust, and commitment, biblical characters take action on the plan God gave them. Rarely did they get the program all at once. Most of the time, it was through blind faith, putting one foot in front of another and they did as they believed they were called to do. Remember, you and I have the Bible in the completed form. The people living out the stories had no idea of the ending, or any real reasoning other than faith to believe it was their duty to do as instructed. That is why you must take something that seems silly, like your life's healthy vision to God in prayer and ask for His instruction. You will get the best-individualized insights that way, and with faith as small as a mustard seed, you can move mountains in your life and health.

Noah may have been the luckiest person in the Bible, in terms of plans provided by God. Read Genesis chapters 6 through 8 on your own to get the full depth of what Noah and his family went through preparing for and enduring the great flood. In Genesis chapter 6, at the ripe age of 500, Noah got detailed dimensions for the ark that he was to build for a storm that was supposed to come. From there, the details continue with the number and types of animals and food to store. What you see throughout chapters 6 and 7 in the book of Genesis is Noah didn't question God's request, but repeatedly did everything just as God commanded him. By chapter 8, Noah had approached 600 years old when the flood finally came, and God fulfilled His promise to Noah for being obedient. Noah and all the wild animals in the ark survived and witnessed the water recede and the land reappear.

Let's think this through in our day. Regardless of how you choose to see the Bible and how it counted age, Noah was mature in years when he first got the instruction from God. Proving no matter your age, you have not missed the boat, pun intended. God can still use you, and you can reap His promises. Those detailed instructions didn't come from a meeting at the local coffee shop, where God pulled up a seat and told Noah to get out his pen and paper and take notes. There are very few moments in the Bible, where God speaks audibly. Meaning, Noah got his instructions during his prayer and quiet time. Knowing God and His Word to the point, Noah couldn't explain his inclinations any other way than instructions from above.

Imagine how the people in Noah's town and even family probably thought as he started walking out this absurd plan. Build a big ole ship, for a big ole flood that is going to wipe out the big ole world. Undoubtedly, he got gossiped about, and people had to think he lost his mind. Yet, he continually did everything just as God commanded. Noah was secure in his faith that friends and family could not persuade him to discredit his quiet time revelations. I pray you too experience that kind of insight into your life and hold onto it no matter what the outside world says about your vision. Lastly, the Bible tells us that it took 100 years for Noah to be validated by the rain.

Explore: Look back over your life and exam milestones you have already accomplished. Do you have a college degree? Have you received promotions at work? Did you start a business from scratch? Have you found true love? Are you a parent? None of those happen overnight. Pick one or two major milestones and plot out the twist and turns your life took before you accomplished the end goal. And if you are still on one of these journeys, be open to seeing that nothing worth having happens overnight.

ENJOY GOOD HEALTH

If you think Noah waited a long time to see God's faithfulness with the flood, wait till you jump into the story of Abraham and the Lord's covenant with him. Continue your extra credit reading in Genesis chapters 15 and 16 to get to know Abraham on a human level. You'll notice at the beginning of chapter 15 that the word of the Lord came to Abraham in a vision.

> *After this, the word of the Lord came to Abraham in a vision: "Do not be afraid, Abraham. I am your shield, your very great reward."—Genesis 15:1 (NIV)*

Abraham, like us, went straight to God with all his shortcomings and inabilities on why God must have his vision all wrong. Back in Abraham's day, having a son was a big deal to carry on the family heritage. If a man did not produce a son, then all that his family had worked for and acquired would go to a distant relative. Not exactly what you wanted to happen. God's covenant with Abraham was two-fold, one that he would have a son of his flesh and blood, and another that his bloodline would be as countless as the stars in terms of future generations. But God's covenant was based on Abraham's willingness to believe and obey.

Do not miss the power in the believing and obeying piece of this story and so many others. God would have remained Abraham's shield, but his very great reward required a partnership in him completing the task handpicked for him. The same goes for you. For Abraham, his first task was to prepare a specific sacrifice for the Lord. Abraham accomplished that to a tee. Next came the waiting that he would bear a son of his own. You've heard this story before, in Genesis chapter 16, Abraham got hasty and tried to take God's promise into his own hands. Allowing frustration and doubts and fear creep in, Abraham and Sara fell off the wagon so-to-speak and got themselves in a heap of trouble. But God didn't forfeit His promise, because they fell short. Once again, Abraham and Sara showed faithfulness in correcting their wrongs to the best they could, and the promise was born.

God promised Abraham and Sara a son, but the process of conception to birth can apply to any area of your life. Parents, whether biological or adoptive, know that there is a whole lot of waiting and unknowns between becoming pregnant to delivery. The same goes for those who choose to adopt to finally arriving on your gotcha day. For natural births, no matter how excited you are to hold that baby and start your family, you can't rush the process. In the beginning, you can hardly tell that a woman is bearing a child, but on the inside countless magnificent actions are being taken to form a life. Over time it is evident to the world that the woman is changing, the baby is growing, and a miracle is on the way. Just because you can't see God working, doesn't mean the seed didn't get planted. You have an enormous amount of work to do, both in the physical world and in the spiritual realm, to prepare you for your promise.

We will never know how much sooner Abraham and Sara would have had Isaac had they not fallen into haste and taken a detour. I've come to learn that pondering the "what if's" of your life's mistakes isn't productive. What is productive is learning from your mishaps and moving forward, back on God's path, and doing your best to stick with Him and His approved vision for your life. If you're reading this book, chances are you've fallen off the wellness wagon a time or twelve. Falling into fad-trends that promise fast results can be alluring and tempting, but they never prove to provide long term success or wellness. The book of Proverbs offers Godly and practical advice about many matters you face in your everyday life. On several accounts, Proverbs points to the importance of having a plan or a vision for success and avoiding quick fixes. This wisdom applies to your health and wellness, too.

> *The plans of the diligent lead to profit, as surely as haste leads to poverty.*
> *Proverbs 21:5 (NIV)*

> *Careful planning puts you ahead in the long run; hurry and scurry puts you further behind. Proverbs 21:5 (The Message)*

Several proverbs praise diligence or persistent effort and the profit or harvest it brings. Keep in mind that even if profit isn't always material, it is still spiritually positive and worth seeking. In Proverbs 21:5, the word haste should be explored more in-depth. Haste means rash actions or desires for a quick return on investment. As a dietitian, I translate this into pills, powders, patches, and fad diet schemes that promise you the world but offer little in the long-term. Jumping into eating patterns because of a celebrity, magazine article, or 90-day challenge at work, will only set you back. Accepting that you need to take time to plan carefully and diligently pursue a path that is right for you will reap a harvest, others will be envious to witness.

ENJOY GOOD HEALTH

Hasty dieting decisions do as much damage to your body as they do to your mind, especially if it leads to "yo-yo" dieting or "weight-cycling." That is where you experience weight loss and weight gain in a short amount of time. You are aware of how emotionally draining this process can become. You can be excited over short-term weight loss and progress, then experience feelings of guilt, shame, and disappointment as the diet starts to fail you. With your tail tucked in defeat, you quickly hop onto the next diet trend to come into town. You're not to blame for falling prey to these quick-fixes. The fad-diet system is rigged to keep you coming back for more. But, after years of yo-yo dieting, your body starts to work against you from the inside out. Without understanding why this approach is counterproductive, you're more likely to keep giving just-one-more promising-fad a try.

When you start to reduce your caloric intake, especially if you are removing carbohydrate calories, the body almost instantly loses weight associated with water retention. Some consumed dietary carbohydrates get stored in the form of glycogen for future energy. For every one gram of carbohydrate stored in the body as glycogen, there are approximately 2-3 grams of water retained. It's a natural process and a simple explanation for why you feel less bloated and shed pounds days after slowing down the consumption of carbohydrates. It is a false sense of progress when most likely, it is a fluid loss. Add in the reduction of sodium found in foods typically "not allowed" on most fad-diets, and you can quickly lose 5-10 pounds in a short period. Of course, this makes you extremely happy!

After a few days or weeks on a lower-carbohydrate diet, you will have exhausted the extra water weight to lose, and progress will stall. Typically, it is the first wave of disappointment. If you were to fall off the wagon at this point, you would quickly regain the water retention with the introduction of carbohydrates or salty foods back into your diet. Whether it is real weight or not, you will be discouraged. Assuming you stick with the program or the low-calorie eating plan for weeks longer, you will start to notice another decrease in weight. The problem with quick weight loss is the pounds lost are most likely coming from your precious muscle mass, not body fat, as you would like to think. There are several reasons the body doesn't just jump into dropping fat tissue; most of it has to do with survival mechanisms. If you were in a real starvation mode, body fat would spare your life much longer than muscle mass.

The saddest metabolic part of losing muscle tissue is you forfeit your calorie-burning machine. When you are not in an aerobic state of moving, walking, or partaking in daily activities, your muscle tissue is what is burning the majority of your calories at rest. For instance, muscle tissue has been shown to burn an estimated seven to ten calories per pound per day, compared to two to three calories per pound per day for fat. In theory, if you replace a pound of fat with a pound of muscle, you can expect to burn more calories. In reverse, when you lose muscle tissue, you lose the ability to burn more calories per pound per day. Unfortunately, fat is retained more quickly than muscle tissue; therefore, when you do fall off the wagon, you gain back fat pounds, not lean mass.

ENJOY GOOD HEALTH

When you tune in with what is going on in your body, you learn how to respond. Listen, our bodies are not in the business of enjoying change. The human body is like homeostasis. Take your temperature; for example, the body works hard to keep you stable at 98.6 degrees. The longer you have lived in a body that is carrying extra weight, the harder your body is going to fight to keep it the way it likes it.

Dieting often does lead to fat loss. However, fat loss leads to decreased levels of the hormone leptin, which usually helps you feel full. Under your regular routine, your fat stores release leptin into the bloodstream. This is your body's signal that energy stores are available, and signals you to eat less and slow down. As you lose body fat, leptin decreases; therefore, your appetite increases. Your body is indicating that it needs to resupply the depleted energy stores you are working very hard to discard. This is compounded by the fact that you've lost muscle mass, so when you overeat, you overstore calories. Sadly, most people who lose weight on a short-term diet end up weighing heavier than before they started the diet. The weight gain may prompt you to begin another cycle of weight loss, but now you are even more muscle deficient with more fat stores. In essence, your hill to climb just got much harder. Not to mention you are emotionally bankrupt and feeling discouraged and disappointed.

If this scenario seems all too familiar to you, do not be dismayed. You can't do better until you know better. With eyes wide open and fully understanding your past and current health status, you can set the stage for real change that is much more rewarding. It is imperative to have a nutrition and exercise plan that supports your overall goals and the preservation of muscle tissue. If you need or want to let go of unnecessary weight take into consideration what might also be at stake for a quick loss, your muscle tissue. Hasty dieting decisions truly lead to poverty, as in Proverbs 21:5. The loss is in your mental and physical capabilities of getting back on the wellness train. Take to heart that rapid weight loss and regain can lead to a host of health consequences. You are better off with a solid plan and slow progress. It is the way God intended most things to happen.

Explore: Think back over your dieting career. Now that you better understand the anatomy and physiology parts to the body letting go of weight, can you see a trend in your own dieting decisions? Sketch out a timeline of your weight ups and downs and what diet trend you were participating in at the moment. See if there are any connections or patterns.

> *We do not want you to become lazy, but to imitate those who through faith and patience inherit what has been promised. Hebrews 6:12 (NIV)*

> *If people can't see what God is doing, they stumble all over themselves; but when they attend to what he reveals, they are most blessed. Proverbs 29:18 The Message (MSG)*

Some theologians claim there are over 3,000 different promises made by God in the Bible. I haven't gone through and highlighted them all, but I did share Noah's and Abrahams's stories that were highly favored by God at the beginning of this chapter. You could add Moses, Ruth, and

Paul to the list, plus countless others that walked with God, imperfectly, but consistently and saw His amazing grace and favor. What I don't want you to miss is that each promise that came to pass was due to the human being having a plan, stepping out in faith, and then pursuing it all the way to the finish line. You must dig in and pursue this plan of better health with hope and grit. No, losing weight or reversing your need for blood pressure medicine doesn't save the world from a flood, or release thousands from bondage in Egypt, but it will produce the results you have been praying to receive.

God is not looking for perfect people to bless. He is looking for people to say, "Yes, Lord. Now what? I'm walking this thing out till the end. Your will, not my own." You may not think that your wellness journey fits the need to have this kind of faith, but remember, God wants all of you, including your desires, to be in better health. He wants your motives to be Holy, and He will challenge your heart along the way. If you wish to play with grandkids or climb a mountain, God knows the desires of your heart. My prayer is that you become like those in the Bible that stayed the course with committed faith and then got everything promised to them.

Our prayer - *Lord, I need you, and I am willing to wait for your power to come. Teach me patience and endurance as I put your plan for my health into action. Help me to see that you are the God who always keeps His word and I can trust that you will show up when the plan doesn't make sense or old behaviors are hard to tame. You redeemed me when I didn't deserve it, and you will come now, too. As I put my plan in action, I will look to you, Lord. Amen.*

Chapter 4
Grit Meets Grace

I will hold myself to a higher standard of grace, not perfection.

By now, you should have a vision for good health and a plan on how to get there. Creating the end and drawing out a plan of action are the easy parts of the process. Go back to Noah's story and imagine him sketching a blueprint of the ark. It would have been easy and understandable for him to tuck those plans in his Bible, counting the cost of the massive undertaking. Many stories in the Bible leave a lot to the imagination, but they are still human, and you can assume they looked at their God-sized visions the same way we do ours. The real work and faith came when Noah went to cut the first log and gathered the helpers needed. Planning is the fun part; the pursuit of that plan is where grit must meet grace.

Most likely, you and I have never met, but I will assume that this isn't your first rodeo when it comes to getting a grip on your dietary habits or relationship with food. Whether you've yo-yo dieted the last several decades, or suffer from body dysmorphia and fatphobia, you've tried to "fix it" in the past. The problem is you're trying to fix the wrong thing: your diet. When what needs repairing is your thinking or mindset. If you're honest, there have already been self-doubt, and a negative mindset creeps in when preparing to make changes. You understand that something has to give, but there seems to be a battle waging inside of you that is determined to keep you from succeeding.

I wish I had a bulletproof response to ending stinking thinking, and set you on a smooth track to guarantee better health and happiness. But life isn't rainbows and butterflies, and good health isn't abs and skinny jeans. The good news is this internal war that has been waging on the inside of you with food and body image is universal and an area to grow in Christ. The bad news is that there is no simple way to pray it away. You must enter the journey with grit, a predetermined mental toughness that you are going to have unyielding courage in the face of your inner heckler, no matter how long this road lasts. And, accept you will need a lot of grace while trying to learn to eat for Jesus and not the world's standard. My only intention is to offer you a sense of peace. You're not alone in the non-stop struggle to resist and redirect your stinking thinking. God is very aware of your bondage, and He has provided you a Helper.

Before a faith-filled Christian can fully begin to tap into the Godlike helper living on the inside, they must first start to recognize who wants to help and who wants to hold back the believer. Apostle Paul appears to wrestle with different versions of his voice inside his head in the seventh chapter of Romans. It can read like a madman is writing it. Once you understand the mental struggle Paul is trying to make sense of, it becomes easy to relate to his struggle while you're trying to successfully change any behavior.

> I do not understand what I do. For what I want to do I do not do, *but what I hate I do. And if I do what I do not*

want to do, I agree that the law is good. As it is, it is no longer I myself who do it, but it is sin living in me. For I know that good itself does not dwell in me, that is, in my sinful nature. For I have the desire to do what is good, but I cannot carry it out. For I do not do the good I want to do, but the evil I do not want to do—this I keep on doing. Now if I do what I do not want to do, it is no longer I who do it, but it is sin living in me that does it. Romans 7:15-20 (NIV)

Poor Paul, like the rest of us, he found himself falling short of perfection, wanting to do what he knew to be right, but feeling like something else would take over, and he would act in opposition. Envision Paul pacing back and forth in a tent, getting anxious with this perplexing mental ping pong game talking to God aloud. I've been there, finding myself talking out loud, saying it seems like something else takes over and defies what I say I desire to do. The point to start to recognize is Paul is discovering and beginning to articulate that there are different parts to our internal makeup. Paul is starting to realize there is a war waging in his mind, and you need to, too. Paul also becomes flooded with guilt and regret for not being strong enough to keep the law perfectly. Sound familiar?

Explore: We all have our wellness weaknesses that seem so ingrained in our personalities or daily routines. It feels impossible to overcome. It's time to purge our food vices on paper. Get real honest with yourself and brainstorm all the ways you feel pigeonholed by your personality. Can you not refuse sweets? Do you find more excuses than reasons to exercise? Do you bail on your healthy lunch you packed for a drive-thru or breakroom freebies? Are you quick to cave in to food temptations? When your emotions peak or plummet, do you find comfort in food? You may be on the other side of the struggle and feel anxious when you're not counting every calorie, or fearful of falsely labeled forbidden foods. You can scribble down quick answers or write out specific scenarios. Remember, you repeat what you don't repair. This exercise should not bring you condemnation, but it's you taking control and bringing light to the dark places holding you back. Allow the Holy Spirit to convict; you will learn how He can help repair it, too.

It is comforting to know that the apostles were humans too. All the greats in the Bible, including Paul, went through the same pulls on the inside. One clear distinction between Bible heroes and us is they were more tapped into detaching their who from their do, and accepting a higher level of grace along the way. Paul's perspective of his internal war is what ultimately gave him the tools to win more times than not and serve the right master and do great things. Christians will unwillingly serve the hated master, and feel powerless to shake off the shackles of the flesh, until they recognize the powerful and gracious Helper, and allow Him to rescue them. You have to surrender to succeed.

> *So I find this law at work: Although I want to do good, evil is right there with me. For in my inner being I delight in God's law; but I see another law at work in me, waging war against the law of my mind and making me a prisoner of the law of sin at work within me. What a wretched man I am! Who will rescue me from this body*

> *that is subject to death? Thanks be to God, who delivers me through Jesus Christ our Lord! So then, I myself in my mind am a slave to God's law, but in my sinful nature a slave to the law of sin. Romans 7:21-25 (NIV)*

You may find it hard to comprehend that this level of Spiritual warfare would be happening over a box of doughnuts, a side of fries, or a half-hour jog around your neighborhood. The ah-ha moment you need to have is that Paul becomes fully aware that the prison he feels trapped in is in his mind, and the only deliverer from his mental bondage is Jesus Christ with help from the Holy Spirit. To get help, you have to be able to recognize the Helper. Believers should spend the rest of their lives trying to become more sensitive to sensing and responding to the Holy Spirit. Christian's Holy Helper. Tap into the Holy Spirit's help at the grocery store, the dinner table, and especially while standing in front of a mirror.

> *So I say, walk by the Spirit, and you will not gratify the desires of the flesh. For the flesh desires what is contrary to the Spirit, and the Spirit what is contrary to the flesh. They are in conflict with each other, so that you are not to do whatever you want. But if you are led by the Spirit, you are not under the law. Galatians 5:16-18 (NIV)*

In the fifth chapter of Galatians, you find Paul still teaching the church the importance of recognizing the two different pieces to a Christian's inner life. He starts to put descriptions of the various parts: flesh and spirit. Flesh in the Bible often describes the fleshy parts of an animal, including humans. It is also a turn of phrase that identifies certain sins as "carnal," which comes from the Latin word caro, carnis, meaning "flesh." To me, I think of flesh as our animal nature. If you have indoor pets, think of how stubborn they are to get whatever it is they want at all costs. Parents go through stages with toddlers and young children seeing an untamed flesh in action over a sippy cup, school shoes, or homework.

Our family had a boxer dog named Brutus, who was highly allergic to chicken. If he ate scraps or even treats made with real chicken, he would break out into a rash and itch like crazy. We did our diligence to remove chicken from his diet and protect him from being exposed. You may fully understand the concern we had for our fur baby if you or a loved one has a severe allergy or intolerance to certain foods or food substances. The difference between humans and pets is at some point, people grow into understanding and accepting their limits and potentially life-threatening responses to certain foods or ingredients and start to cooperate. Pets never get it. No matter how lousy chicken would make Brutus feel after consumption, he never stopped begging or trying to find a way to sneak scraps of meals made with chicken. Brutus's story can be an excellent metaphor for how an untamed flesh will act without spiritual maturity of hearing and responding to the Holy Spirit's direction.

Untamed desires of your flesh often clash with the Spirit. The urges of the Spirit usually contradict your flesh. You can spot your ego or flesh anytime your feelings or emotions are trying to urge you to edge God out of a situation or your decision making. Regardless of the terminology you choose to use; the Bible is clear that there is a conflict happening. Flesh and Spirit routinely disagree. Where there is conflict, there are two sides to consider. There are two separate entities in conflict with each other on the inside of your brain. And yes, the war wages over your food choices which can range from overeating to over-analyzing every calorie. To your body image thoughts, and ultimately your desire or lack of to take care of your Holy vessel.

But if the Spirit leads you, you are not under the law (vs. 18) is the gold nugget lesson to learn and spend your energy trying to become more sensitive to responding too. The word led is critical. Where something causes a person to go along with another by way of hand-holding or authority is to lead. You can think of your Spirit as a personal guide or commander in chief, leading you daily. As Brutus's owners, we knew what was best for him regardless of his desires. We would lead him through mealtime by providing him with safe choices. Parents and guardians do the same with children. It is our job to lead, guide, and nudge them through life to ultimately make sound and righteous decisions. I'll be the first to admit, guiding and protecting our pets is much easier than raising humans or hearing and responding to the Spirit correctly. Humans are the most robust breed to break fleshy habits.

In Galatians 5: 19-21, you can read a laundry list of acts of the flesh. It includes but is not limited to everything from sexual immorality, debauchery, idolatry, discord, jealousy, anger, selfish ambition, envy, and more. These Bible verses offer a stern warning that those who live with those desires in control will not inherit the kingdom of God. Harsh warnings to digest, but don't overlook how the desires of our flesh can pop up into any aspect of life, including our wellness journey. Now, this is an excellent time to pause and make some things very clear. I need you to fully understand that eating and enjoying food of any kind is not a sin. Going back for a second helping isn't automatically sinful. Fried foods, sugary beverages, and decadent desserts are not devil worship. Your physical health or outward appearance is not tied in any way to your salvation! Re-read those statements until the cows come home, and it sinks in.

Where the lines can get blurry, and you may find that the Holy Spirit convicts, but never condemns you is when your love or desire for certain foods or body images become out of balance. When you are out of balance, you have forfeited your freedom and feel trapped. Debauchery includes excessive indulgence in sensual pleasures, including food, beverage, and exercise. That can be too much soda to too much organic, fresh-pressed orange juice. Both drinks in extremes will have negative impacts on your health. Idolatry includes the worship of idols. Losing weight can become an idol whether you are successful at it or not. Exercise or sport can become an idol if you spend more energy worshiping your appearance or athletic abilities than you do God. Hatred and jealousy that manifests in you comparing your body, health report or food choices to others become spiritually dangerous.

Explore: Take an honest timeout and get real with yourself and confess some stuffed feelings. At times do you think more about food and your figure than you do about God and His Glory? Have you ever found yourself a little mad at

God for not giving you the desired worldly genes that are deemed attractive? Are you angry that you developed a chronic illness, food allergies, or worse? Get it all out. You have permission to vent. God hears you and isn't here to condemn you or your raw, fleshy feelings. At your core, you're still an animal, like our beloved Brutus, wanting chicken even though it will make you itch.

> But the fruit of the Spirit is love, joy, peace, forbearance, kindness, goodness, faithfulness, gentleness and self-control. Against such things there is no law. Those who belong to Christ Jesus have crucified the flesh with its passions and desires. Since we live by the Spirit, let us keep in step with the Spirit. Galatians 5:22-25 (NIV)

Let's balance out this emotional rollercoaster with some positive energy. Hopefully, you just dumped out some hard emotions, thoughts, and feelings connected to your human flesh. Now, let's keep reading our Bibles and see there is a light to this darkness, and it is the form of the Spirit. Paul details the desires of the flesh in Galatians 5 and then counters it with the fruits of the Spirit: love, joy, peace, forbearance, kindness, goodness, faithfulness, gentleness, and self-control. He also reiterates that Christ's-followers have already defeated the flesh and its desires through His crucifixion and resurrection. Rounding out the positive message with instructions that since we live by the Spirit, let us keep in step with the Spirit.

Notice the wording, that let us keep in step with the Spirit (vs. 25) signals you are to walk alongside the Spirit, as a guide would lead the blind, or parent a small child across the street by hand. Paul is making the connection that Christians have the choice to walk and live in the Spirit, and by making that choice, you will not fulfill the lust of the flesh that tempts and torments us. But if the Spirit leads you, you are not under the law. When you are living life and making food and fitness decisions with Godly intentions, you need not worry about the legality of perfection.

> *By their fruit you will recognize them. Do people pick grapes from thorn bushes, or figs from thistles? Likewise, every good tree bears good fruit, but a bad tree bears bad fruit. A good tree cannot bear bad fruit, and a bad tree cannot bear good fruit. Every tree that does not bear good fruit is cut down and thrown into the fire. Thus, by their fruit you will recognize them. Matthew 7:16-20 (NIV)*

It is one thing to understand you should be walking with and led by the Spirit, and it is another thing to start implementing it into your everyday life. First, you must learn to recognize the prompting of the Spirit to follow it. In Matthew 17, you learn to understand the difference between the flesh and Spirit by its fruit. Bring this lesson into your everyday life by analyzing thoughts, actions, and outcomes by their fruit. When thought patterns about food, your body, or the wellness process don't provoke the fruits of the Spirit, that's not your Helper in your head. If particular longtime food and lifestyle habits haven't reaped good health in your life, then it isn't helping. Staying in relationships with people who are continually belittling your efforts, your looks, or your style aren't there to sharpen you.

Once you start to recognize the fruit that is coming from the different avenues of your life, you have to take the next step of the process: pruning. Every tree that does not bear good fruit is cut down and thrown into the fire (vs. 19). Thoughts, actions, habits, routines, and your environment are all trees to consistently and continuously be subject to fruit analysis. Creating your healthy vision for your life is non-negotiable. It will be your benchmark for what to prune and know what to keep. You can't prune your garden based on multiple influences' blueprints. When any part of your daily life starts to bear fruit that doesn't align with the fruits of the Spirit or your healthy vision, throw it out. Physically stop doing it or physically remove it. You can assess whether your lifestyle is healthy or not by its fruit.

> *Remain in me, as I also remain in you. No branch can bear fruit by itself; it must remain in the vine. Neither can you bear fruit unless you remain in me. "I am the vine; you are the branches. If you remain in me and I in you, you will bear much fruit; apart from me you can do nothing. John 15:4-5 (NIV)*

The million-dollar question you are probably pondering is how do you stay well connected to the promptings of the Holy Spirit so you can bear the fruit of the Spirit? In John 15, Jesus answers this burning question. It is easy to comprehend how, if you cut off a berry branch from the vine, that plant will not bear any good fruit ever again. The same goes for Christians.

If you and I cut ourselves off from Jesus, there is no way to absorb His nourishment and help. You will not be successful at making significant lifestyle and behavior changes without staying connected to your grace outlet. Nor will you be able to enjoy the journey or enjoy good health without a deep and intimate relationship with Jesus as your top priority. Jesus told us that His joy might be in us so that our satisfaction may be complete (John 15:11).

In other words, to walk by the Spirit (Galatians 5:16), you must abide in the vine (John 15:5). Effective practices that keep you securely united with Christ on your wellness journey include plenty of quiet and prayer time—worshiping God more than worrying over your weight. Worshiping God in your kitchen, in your closet, and in front of your bathroom mirror. Recognize that the fruit of the Spirit is singular and not plural. You are connected to the Spirit when you experience love for yourself and find joy in what you eat. You are at peace with the wellness process and are patient with your progress. You show kindness towards your body, by using good self-talk, and are faithful to your healthy vision. You develop a gentleness in how you handle missteps and begin to exude self-control. If any of these are out of balance, you are not entirely in step with the Spirit.

Explore: Return to your wellness weakness. Take quality quiet time and prayerfully examine your list for ways to implement the fruit of the Spirit into each. Begin to pray for more self-love, joy, peace, self-patience, kind self-talk, and a higher standard of grace as you learn self-control. Avoid turning the page to the next chapter without completing this task.

ENJOY GOOD HEALTH

Do you not know that your bodies are temples of the Holy Spirit, who is in you, whom you have received from God? You are not your own; you were bought at a price. Therefore honor God with your bodies. 1 Corinthians 6:19-20

I share these verses in 1 Corinthians reluctantly because I feel they have been unintentionally used to shame believers into thinking if they're not skinny, eating vegetables, or avoiding added sugars, they aren't caring for their body appropriately. Or if you find yourself managing a chronic illness or cancer, you've been punished. Not true. What is true is that our bodies are a temple or a vessel for God's work to be carried out. Taking care of it only makes sense, but nudged into dieting through the use of guilt isn't helping you or the kingdom. When I read these verses, I see it as an opportunity to take care of something higher than me. As a mom, that resonates with me and puts me in a position of protecting or nurturing God's temple, versus disappointing Him with my lack of willpower.

I've had the great privilege of two healthy pregnancies. Each time I found out I was pregnant, it was like a switch went off on the inside, and I knew that I couldn't allow my disordered eating patterns to affect the baby's potential to grow and be well-nourished. My relationship with food is at its best when I'm pregnant. I eat well, and for the right reasons. It was after I gave birth that old mindsets and body image issues would creep back in and try to take root. It wasn't until God showed me in 1 Corinthians that my body is still not my own, and that I had a duty to do well by it for Christ's sake. I started viewing how I thought about my body, fed my body, and used my body differently. No, it's not the same as being physically pregnant, but the idea that it isn't all about me helped me care for my body in a way, I don't think I could if it was just me, living for me.

Here is the hard truth. If believers are to be the Temple of the Spirit, we will have to give up the right of ownership to God. As long as you are the owner, things will go your way, not His, which includes what you eat, drink, and how you choose to move, rest, and respect your body. The plan is for us to conform to His promptings, not the other way around. As long as we allow our appetites and insecurities to stay in charge, the Spirit is limited. Think of how many times God prompted you to do something differently, but you weren't comfortable being uncomfortable, so you bailed on it. You can't know what God intends for your diet, exercise, or self-esteem until you commit to self-denial and dialing into His Word. Combine that with ample worship and quiet time, and you'll start to know His voice and heed His call. That's when you have grit and grace to live out your God-inspired wellness lifestyle.

It is good to note that procrastination and a passive response to doing what we know we should, in terms of our health, is also a tool of Satan. There is no point in putting off taking care of yourself. The more passive you are, the more our flame for following God's promptings diminish. Passive people wait to be moved by an outside force before finally taking action. But you are to be motivated and led by the Holy Spirit, who has probably already been knocking at your heart's door for some time about your mindset and well-being habits.

The best way to be on guard against the spirit of passivity is to do what you need to do now, and do it with a thankful heart.

Our prayer: *God, I confess I am not able and that in my humanness I often waiver. I cannot be and do all the pieces to create a balanced and healthy life alone. Only with your great power and the Holy Spirit can I achieve our healthy vision. Help me to surrender my wellness weaknesses and completely depend on your perfect power and presence. Give me the courage to continue forward and rely on you. Amen.*

Chapter 5
Your Wellness Thief

The thief comes only in order to steal and kill and destroy. I came that they may have and enjoy life, and have it in abundance [to the full, till it overflows]—John 10:10 (AMP)

Prayerfully, I hope you are starting to connect some dots in your pursuit of better health, or journey to find freedom from food obsession. In the intro, I stated that a lot of us have allowed our thoughts and feelings around food and self-image to cloud our higher purpose that our Creator has intended for us. As a registered dietitian, a woman, and a bonafide Christian, I believe now more than ever that one of Satan's most significant accomplishments in the Western World is creating the skinny smokescreen. This smokescreen is a cultural cloud that blinds women of their real call and purpose with unrealistic views of health and happiness.

God started wrestling with my outlook on health and wellness while I was on a spiritual quest to free myself from connecting my worth to my weight. It's been a long road, and I joyfully can say I am on the other side of the storm, but not out of the boat. When I think I've got stinkin' thinkin' about food and my physical appearance beat, life enters a new challenging season: bearing children, balancing family, work, and a consistent fitness routine. I've accepted that body image issues and controlling food intake will be a lifelong opportunity to grow closer to Jesus.

God provided a fresh perspective on John 10:10, and it helped me to better understand my unhealthy attachment to body image and food control. Regardless of the Bible version you choose to read, John 10:10 provides the same scene. Like a thief in the night, Satan is looking to steal joy from you. Christians get too caught up in the devil wanting to disrupt the big stuff in our life: marriage, kids, finances, pornography, or world war. True, evil has a death grip on our culture in unimaginable ways that are wreaking havoc on our nation and the world. I am not undermining any of the big stuff. But don't overlook the notion that the devil is in the small, everyday details, too.

It is a fool's mistake to think that thieves only exist to steal the big ticketed items. You are more likely to have smaller items taken from your property than a home invasion. You are sorely mistaken if you don't think the devil cares about how you feel about food and your thighs. When you stand in front of a mirror and downgrade yourself, that's stealing and killing your joy. After eating a slice of pizza, going back for seconds, or succumbing to a food temptation and then spending hours self-shaming and wallowing in a sea of guilt, that's stealing and killing your joy. When our daughters and sons bear witness to us belittling ourselves or worse others for food choices or for the way one looks, that's killing the next generations' chance to break free from the wellness addiction and stealing their joy before they ever had a chance to find it.

Explore: If you've never thought about your thoughts being the devil's playground, you might be a little emotional at the moment. That is okay. I still get choked up, and a little angry when I think about getting duked by the devil in my head. Take some time to pinpoint the thoughts and feelings around food and your body image that has sucked the joy from your daily life. Do you find yourself anxious over meals? Do you get angry when you think about fixing "healthy" foods over what you would prefer to eat? Do you avoid mirrors, shopping, or are you constantly comparing your body to others? Have you avoided fun activities such as open invitations, water days, or summer outings because you don't want to wear the appropriate clothes?

> *Be alert and of sober mind. Your enemy the devil prowls around like a roaring lion looking for someone to devour.*
> *1 Peter 5:8 (NIV)*

Peter, a disciple with one of the greatest redemption stories ever recorded in the Bible, understood that there was a thief after his newfound joy in Christ. He portrayed Satan as a roaring lion, on the prowl looking for someone to devour and he warned believers to be alert and of sober mind. You can take the definition of sober to heart and be assured that regardless of your view on alcohol, you're less likely to make wise food decisions when under-the-influence or while recovering from a few too many adult beverages. But moving past that surface-level notion of sober and understanding the word also means clear-headed. Plenty of things can cloud your mind and make decision making difficult, like, your rollercoaster of emotions from happy to sad, mad, confused, concerned, conflicted, and beyond. To your mental state of whether you are well-rested, exhausted, stressed, or spread too thin. Connect these vital dots: the state of your mind determines the devil's ability to have a foothold directing your daily decisions.

The devil doesn't care about what you eat for dinner, whether you skipped the doughnuts or the size of your thighs. But Satan does care that you care. Your sensitivity to your weight, health, and body image becomes a weak spot for him to attack your joy on a daily basis. He will send temptations, trails, and whisper in your ear hurtful thoughts to keep your eyes off the real prize. As long as you are on the hamster wheel of unattainable wellness, you're forfeiting your ability to enjoy good health and, ultimately, Jesus to the fullest. The Apostle Paul understood what Peter was warning against, but his perspective is what helped change the game for me, and hopefully you, too.

> *Therefore, in order to keep me from becoming conceited, I was given a thorn in my flesh, a messenger of Satan, to torment me. Three times I pleaded with the Lord to take it away from me. But he said to me, "My grace is sufficient for you, for my power is made perfect in weakness." Therefore I will boast all the more gladly about my weaknesses, so that Christ's power may rest on me. That is why, for Christ's sake, I delight in weaknesses, in insults, in hardships, in persecutions, in difficulties. For when I am weak, then I am strong. 2 Corinthians 12:7-10 (NIV)*

How many times have you prayed for God to melt the fat away? Maybe that wasn't your exact prayer, but if you've ever disliked the body you dwell in, I'm sure there have been some silent prayers for a diet to work finally or for the desire for sweets to cease or your latest "as seen on TV" workout miracle to be from heavenly places. God is the miracle master, but miracles don't keep us happy. Just ask the Israelites who witnessed a sea part, received manna, quail from nowhere, and water from rocks. Yet, they still kept begging for more miracles and were unhappy. Repeat after me: Miracles don't mature you in Christ.

ENJOY GOOD HEALTH

Have you ever stopped to think that your struggle with weight, certain foods, or self-discipline could be your thorn to experience Godly grace? Paul understood that being human means having weaknesses and the need for an unending supply of grace. Paul refers to his weaknesses as a thorn in his flesh, a pesky little thing that never quite goes away and always can get flared up under the right circumstances. It can feel as if Satan is tormenting you with that thorn at times. It is doubtful that weight or body image is your only thorn, but that is what we are focused on here. I certainly know what it is like to have triggers that flare up insecurities, ignite emotional eating, and drinking decisions. The pivoting point is recognizing these thorns as opportunities, not burdens.

Opportunities to lean into Jesus and trust the Holy Spirit will guide through the wave of emotions, the dressing room, the dining experience, or beach trip. Instead of going to God in despair because you don't see the results you want, go to God for guidance and strength to make healthier decisions. Healthier decisions could be choosing a salad over French fries, but it could also be to put on the bathing suit and join your family in the water without the crippling fear of what others think. It could be relaxing and enjoying planning meals for your family, asking for encouragement and excitement to try new foods or new cooking methods. The point is there is a shift in how you perceive the situation at hand.

When you are feeling weak, you can be assured that God will be strong. And ultimately, who will get the glory for the change in your life? Do not overlook the chance to praise God privately and publicly when you start to see real changes mentally and/or physically. If you have been struggling for decades with sticking to any sort of balanced eating approach and you finally are kicking tail and taking down pounds, praise the One who is helping you. Learning to let go of worldly ideals of what your thighs should look like and allowing yourself to love your curves or silhouette is a chance to shout from the mountain tops that God is good. Each and every victory in your journey to enjoying good health is a win for you and the Holy Spirit as a team.

The devil doesn't care about the size of your thighs any more than Jesus. Sure, our Heavenly Father wants us to upkeep the vessel He gave you to be healthy and strong, but He is far less worried about the size of it than the condition of its heart. But like Satan, Jesus does care that you care about your body image. That is why He has created the door for you to see Him through your weakness and worries. You may carry this thorn your entire life, but you will get stronger in being triggered by it and find yourself standing firm and steadfast in places you never thought possible.

> *Resist him, standing firm in the faith, because you know that the family of believers throughout the world is undergoing the same kind of sufferings. And the God of all grace, who called you to his eternal glory in Christ, after you have suffered a little while, will himself restore you and make you strong, firm and steadfast. To him be the power for ever and ever. Amen. 1 Peter 5:9-11 (NIV)*

As long as you're on this planet, you will be faced with taming the flesh. Our flesh will always try to fill its own emptiness with outside things and do it best to avoid turning to God. It's just the internal makeup of being human. If enjoying good health for a lifetime appears too daunting, remember that you aren't called to live it out by yourself. When you feel that war is waging on the inside over what to eat for dinner, remember you're not crazy. Your job is not to defeat the flesh. Your only job is to walk in the Spirit. Humble yourself before your dietary decisions and wardrobe woes and ask for Holy Help even if that help is just for today.

God provided for the Israelites in their greatest times of need by sending them mana daily. He didn't allow them to store up food or favor for more than 24 hours. I believe this was to teach them to rely on God every single solitary day. In the beginning, you're only going to be strong enough to handle one day at a time of making some serious changes in your mindsets and lifestyles. Begin now accepting that you will probably not feel like you can handle small changes over a long period of time. The first time you ask for unsweet tea or water over soda, it's going to be awful. The first time you get your chicken grilled over fried, your flesh will have a fit. The first time you pick out an outfit because you feel good in it and not worry about what size it is, you'll fight back old mindsets. Just know you just have to do it one time at a time.

When your Spirit is heavy with the day ahead, repeat to yourself, "Just for today." It's a powerful, yet simple concept that you are strong enough to do anything, just for this 24-hours. Often we are weighed down with anxieties, doubts, and fears. You don't have to muster up the courage to conquer the next five years, five months, or five days. Just focus on the next five minutes of this day.

Explore: Make a list of your "just for today mantras" on a beautiful sticky note or card stock. You can even journal them in your bible by a verse or passage that will be a reminder that your thorns are your opportunities. If you journal daily, add in a "just for today" line to fill in to keep you focused. I'll share a few wellness favorites that have helped me along the way.

Just for today:
I will let go of my worries about my weight.
I will find joy in the clothes in my closet.
I will be grateful for nourishing my body with God's best foods.
I will focus my thoughts on Jesus and not the scale.
I will drink plenty of water.
I will move with a purpose for 20 minutes.
I will eat something green.
I will take my lunch.
I will have faith in myself.
I will check in on my inner peace, more than my social media feed.

It's only fair to warn you how the Holy Spirit works in your life. Especially once you start to see some results and make improvements in your health and wellness mindsets and behaviors. Like any muscle, the more you use it, the stronger it gets, and the more aware you become of the promptings. This is a good thing! However, once the Holy Spirit helps you get fairly strong in one area of wellness, it'll move onto another one. Buckle up; it's just part of the awesome journey of walking hand in hand with God's chosen Helper.

Remember, the devil doesn't stop just because you decide to make improvements in your life. In my experience, the enemy revs up the pressure when you start to get serious about changing your thoughts or lifestyle. You've heard the phrase that the enemy doesn't care about who you are but who you could become. It's true. Just think how powerful the

Western world could be against darkness if we were all healthy and strong in the Holy Spirit. You must be of sober mind and on the lookout. Taking it one day at a time and celebrating the small victories and moving past the insignificant failures. Every minute of every day is a new 60-seconds to think and act differently.

By no means am I suggesting that your co-workers, family, or friends who bring pastries, invite you to parties, or encourage unhealthy living are the devil's partners in crime. It's the thoughts that get provoked when you see the cake in the breakroom that becomes the open door. You will never live in a world without temptation. Even Jesus was tempted while on earth. Removing temptations should not be your top priority. Learning to navigate them with Jesus in mind is the ultimate goal. The underlying theme is Christians should strive to live a life that brings glory to God (1 Corinthians 10:31), and that includes what you choose to eat and how you choose to take care of your body, too. Give God all the glory as you learn to enjoy good health.

You've got this, even if it is just for today!

Our prayer - *God, today is ultimately yours. You made it, you gave it, and I trust you will bless it. Help me to let it go into your hands and lean into your promptings for how I should respond to this the day. May your voice have more power in my mind than my own. It's your day anyway, God, so you take it. Amen.*

Chapter 6
Give Your Mouth a Detox

Fools care nothing for thoughtful discourse; all they do is run off at the mouth
—Proverbs 18:2 (MSG)

Thin became "in" during the 1920s, and since then, Americans have been counting calories in the battle to lose weight. Fast forward a hundred years, and anyone with a smartphone can get a minute by minute scientific breakdown of macro and micronutrients of what they are about to eat or just ate through apps. Countless hours are wasted counting grams and ounces of food, and precious joy is forfeited by having anxious thoughts and feelings about measuring and weighing food to meet numerical nutrition benchmarks set by an algorithm. Charts, graphs, and forecasted food analysis are at your fingertips, yet it still hasn't fixed your relationship with food. In most cases, the more perceived information you have at your fingertips about food, the more unsettled you become at mealtimes.

The next phase of your journey to find freedom and live a healthy life is to watch your mouth for more than calories in. What comes out of your mouth plays a significant role in your overall well-being. It would do you a lot of good to start to think about what you think about. Listen to what you say about yourself, your current wellness situation, and your potential to change. Before you succeed at changing how you eat, you must retrain your self-talk. Everyone wants a magic pill or potion to detox the body, gaining the upper edge to jumpstarting better health. The only detox worthy of your time is one of your toxic self-talk. Let's aim to rid the mouth and mind of thoughts, words, feelings, and beliefs that have undesirable short- and long-term effects on your health and happiness.

Being a registered dietitian, I have heard every grumble, complaint, and harmful speech possible about the foods that heal and nourish. If I had a penny for every perceived "can't" haves, and opinions you have about your body, I'd be rich. It is one of the most depressing parts of trying to work with people on creating a life full of health and joy. I am convinced that corrupt self-conversation causes a lot of health problems and loss of happiness. In Chapter 4, you are encouraged to strengthen the Holy Spirit's voice in your life and lean into His promptings. Christians are told to distinguish between the flesh and the Holy Spirit by its fruit. Remember, if it isn't rooted in love, joy, peace, forbearance, kindness, goodness, faithfulness, guiltlessness, or self-control, it isn't the fruit of the Spirit.

The tongue has the power of life and death, and those who love it will eat its fruit
—*Proverbs 18:21 (NIV)*

Words kill, words give life; they're either poison or fruit— you choose
—*Proverbs 18:21 (MSG)*

Proverbs 18:21 makes it clear that your words are either poison or fruit. What you say to yourself, about yourself, and your food choices will have consequences. The Message version of this verse suggests that it is your choice whether your words create life or death. This can easily cause you conflict, but I hope it also liberates you. Taking inventory of our self-talk can be uncomfortable, but it is also something we can all do. You may not be able to run a marathon, grow organic produce, or cook from scratch, but you and I can be accountable for what comes out of our mouth. Once you fully embrace the weapon that is your words, you will start to manifest positive shifts in your well-being. No, you can't speak yourself thin, attractive, or athletic. But, you certainly can start to heal your relationship with your body and food by cultivating a positive mental environment.

It's time you start to think of words as nutrients, too. You are so quick to try and find foods and ingredients and label them "toxic" or "poison," but there is more to your well-being than what's on your plate. Complaining and grumbling words carry destructive power. When you spend all day talking about what you can't do, what you despise eating, what you desperately miss eating, and how your image brings you to shame, it guarantees you will self-destruct and self-sabotage. Complaining pollutes your mind, and pollution is basically poison surrounding your ability to manifest any thought or action inspired by the fruit of the Spirit. It has been said that the mind can only have one thought at a time. As Proverbs 18:21 shows us, it is up to us whether that singular thought in any given moment is poison or fruitful.

ENJOY GOOD HEALTH

Those of you who constantly complain about the habits and daily decisions it takes to prevent or manage chronic disease, or reach a healthy weight tend to be quite bitter. Don't believe me, recount your self talk about ordering broccoli over French fries, getting in your water ounces, or getting up early to exercise. You might even start listing out every excuse possible why getting healthy is just too hard. No wonder you are not making progress in your health purist with a mind diseased with bitterness. For those on the other end of the spectrum, you may not be bitter, but fearful of letting go of control and actually eating a dessert, or skipping the exercise to enjoy a spontaneous life moment. Either way, your inner voice is creating such a storm your inner being can't see past it to move past it.

Explore: What about the wellness journey that makes you bitter, angry, or fearful? Chances are your internal heckler that wreaks havoc on your self-talk is mad about having to do, eat, or avoid certain things. Or afraid of what others may think. Take time to vent on paper. God knows your heart anyway, so getting out in the open what is eating at you about what you "should" be eating is often therapeutic. You'll hear me repeat several times that you can't fix what you won't acknowledge. What about the wellness culture or wellness journey that causes your blood to boil?

I hope that the brain dump of bitterness was cathartic. It's worth mentioning again not to allow those negative feelings or realization of your hurtful thoughts to get you down. Remember, it is our choice of what to think. Let's all agree you don't want to think those thoughts any longer. They are not serving you or your health well. Now that you have identified the thief thoughts stealing your joy and hampering your progress, you can start to cast those down and replace them with helpful and more fruitful ideas. But be warned, this is where the rubber meets the road, and some sweat equity comes into play. Thinking differently is simple, but it isn't always easy.

A calm and peaceful and tranquil heart is life and health to the body...
Proverbs 14:30 (AMP)

A soothing tongue [speaking words that build up and encourage] is a tree of life... Proverbs 15:4 (AMP)

According to Proverbs, a calm mind is a health to the body. I'd go further to say it is much healthier than a thigh-gap or conquering a fitness feat. And speaking words that build yourself up and provide encouragement on this wellness journey is the ultimate tree of life. Accept the fact that your words can heal. Changing the way you talk, will change the way you respond, which will change your life. You can't heal your body long-term without healing your mind. Negative speech about yourself and the real foods that God gave us to improve and nourish us from long days of serving our families, communities, and thriving pollutes our lives and willpower. With the same vigor, you search for foods to ban or demonize, you should also be searching for destructive thoughts, mindsets, and stinking thinking. If you're at a loss at how to turn the tide and create a soothing tongue, then start with the easiest form of positive talk: thanksgiving.

ENJOY GOOD HEALTH

Speaking and showing gratitude has multiple proven benefits: physical, mental, and spiritual. Even science suggests that gratitude is strongly and consistently associated with greater happiness. A spirit of thanksgiving helps you feel more positive emotions, deal with adversity, and improve overall health. The Bible encourages Christians to create a spirit of gratitude. Throughout his teaching, Apostle Paul demonstrated what it looks like to live a life of gratitude. He wrote, "Show yourselves thankful," and he "thanked God unceasingly." (Colossians 3:15; 1 Thessalonians 2:13).

Believers are taught to bless their food before eating it. Regardless of what is on the plate, you've probably created the habit of blessing the food for the nourishment of your body and your body to His service. Our children learn God is good, God is great. Let us thank Him for our food. By His hands, we are fed. Give us Lord our daily bread. But the question becomes, is this just lip service as a Christian duty, or do you fully embrace what it means to eat with thanksgiving. Lasting positive effects come from having a grateful disposition, not merely saying thank you through gritted teeth. It takes a temperament of thanksgiving to protect you from feelings of entitlement, envy, and resentment, which robs us of joy in life.

> *For everything God created is good, and nothing is to be rejected if it is received with thanksgiving, because it is consecrated by the word of God and prayer.—1 Timothy 4:4-5 (NIV)*

In chapter one, you learned a quick overview of the progression of biblical food laws from the Old to the New Testament. Before Christ, there were strict dietary laws; for example, no pork was given for specific religious and, potentially, health concerns of that day. For example, pork was shunned because it was understood that, if undercooked, it could lead to roundworms, or Trichinosis, migrating to the heart and causing death. Other cultural food laws were often created as a result of what we now understand to be poor food-safety measures. The New Testament, however, tells us that keeping Old Testament food laws for religious reasons is no longer required. Food rules are no longer needed to draw us nearer to God. Paul spent a lot of time battling old traditions with new believers after the resurrection. In the early church, there were false teachers who held on to past mindsets and told Christ-followers to abstain from certain foods. Paul refuted their teachings by reassuring new believers that everything God created is good, and nothing has to be rejected if received with thanksgiving.

> *But food does not bring us near to God; we are no worse if we do not eat, and no better if we do.—1 Corinthians 8:8 (NIV)*

The Bible makes it clear that whatever you choose to eat or to drink that was created by God is good. Every meal and beverage should be consumed with thanksgiving and looked at as a gift for nourishment and enjoyment. God does not see food as "good" or "bad," so neither should you. That doesn't mean that you can eat whatever you want and not have health consequences. It means that no matter what is on your plate, you consume it from a place of gratitude. If it is a big bowl of ice cream, then enjoy every bite and give thanks for the delicious treat. When you make a choice to order a salad over pizza slices, give thanks for the healing nutrients you are consuming and what colorful fruits and vegetables can do for your well-being.

Blessing your food out of routine and then grumbling and complaining about having to eat rabbit food, or envying the smell of a stranger's plate at the table next, is not true gratitude. Coming in after an emotional day and eating everything but the kitchen sink, so-to-speak, and then self-shaming the rest of the night is not being thankful. You can't be truly grateful to consume fruits and vegetables and drink clean water and then step onto a scale only to grip about a lack of progression. On the other end of the spectrum, feeling a sense of superiority because you skip dessert every time, never use oil, always meet your macronutrient goals, and pride yourself for your pants size doesn't mean you're living with a grateful disposition either.

Real freedom to eat healthy means you receive whatever you choose to put on your plate as a gift with genuine appreciation. There is plenty to be grateful for in the West when it comes to food, whether it is fried chicken or an organic meatless panini. Think of the farmer, the animal who sacrificed their lives, the systems in place in the United States to keep your food safe for consumption, the cooks, the wait staff, and on and on. When you do choose plant-based foods, you are sincerely eating out of God's great medicine cabinet, and every bite offers protective nutrients that heal and help you thrive. The main point Paul is trying to make is our food choices do not make us more righteous. You certainly can choose to refuse to eat certain things on the basis of health or serving you or your health well. Now that you have identified personal ethics, but know that it will not give you greater spirituality unless it is consumed with authentic thanksgiving.

> And God said, "Behold, I have given you every plant yielding seed that is on the face of all the earth, and every tree with seed in its fruit. You shall have them for food."—Genesis 1:29 (ESV)

In *Mind Over Fork,* I share why quality over quantity of food matters. I've often found when providing basic nutrition education that the recipient is more likely to be responsive to my recommendations if they understand what is going on inside their bodies. I firmly believe once you understand how whole foods nourish you, you're less likely to complain about having to eat rabbit food. This book isn't geared to promote any specific eating pattern or plan, but I can't discredit the potential healing and nourishment that can come from a lifestyle that includes fruits, vegetables, and wholegrains as a primary staple.

Phytochemicals are found in plant foods such as fruits, vegetables, beans, and whole grains. Other common names for phytochemicals are antioxidants, flavonoids, phytonutrients, flavones, isofalvones, catchins, and polyphenols. These precious nutrients are your body's worker bees and do a really good job at fighting disease and boosting your immune system. Think of your immune system as your guardian angels, hidden out of sight, but there to jump to your defense against germs and other nasty invaders. You want to keep our immune systems as strong as possible. Jesus didn't have weak guardian angels and neither do you!

ENJOY GOOD HEALTH

This excerpt is taken out of Mind Over Fork, you can purchase the book to read the chapter in its entirety. My hope is that it will inspire you to look at the plant kingdom God gave us as a wealth of nourishment that should be received with thanksgiving and great respect.

It may surprise you but an empty stomach does not trigger the hunger drive. The efficient and active digestion and absorption of nutrients from food does. Here is a bare-bones explanation of how digestion works.

We eat food. Our stomach breaks it down into the macronutrients; proteins, fats and carbohydrates. Next, food enters the small intestines and is further broken down into vitamins and minerals, these are your body's worker bees, ready to repair and replenish. Then the small intestines allow the nutrients to be absorbed into the bloodstream and sent to the liver where they will be stored or sent to other parts of the body. What's left is sent to the large intestine where the remaining water is absorbed from the food and then compounded into solid waste to be expelled from the body.

Meanwhile, the nourishment that passed through the small intestine into the bloodstream is busy nourishing the body. Those worker bees, or nutrients from your food, spring into action doing what they were created to do for a working system: maintenance. As absorption is accomplished blood-sugar levels drop and a signal to the brain is sent. The red-alert is triggered that food is needed. At last, it is blood sugar dropping, not the empty stomach, that signals hunger. Stabilize your blood sugar and delay hunger.

Bottom line, the more nutrient dense a food is the more nutrition available to be delivered throughout the body. You can stay well-nourished, full, and satisfied on fewer calories. Calories from processed foods deliver little nutrition and the body will continue the hunger cycle until it attains the nutrients it desires. Or think of it this way, the body will keep asking for food until all the work is done. Junk food gives your large intestines a workout since little is absorbed in the small intestines for any good use. It's best to choose packaged items with legible ingredients; or better yet eat whole foods (fruits, vegetables, whole grains, lean meats, seafood, nuts, seeds and low-fat dairy foods) the way nature intended in whole form.

Explore: Go back to your vent session on what about the wellness culture or wellness journey that causes your blood to boil. Now let's respond to our internal bitterness with a new perspective. Rewrite your nagging thoughts to read as a positive response. It may be hard, or some plant-based foods may not be as tasty, and the weight may not just fall off as fast as you would like it to. It may be scary to eat the doughnut or skip the workout for a good reason. But there is a helpful approach to these perceived roadblocks than just grumbling and complaining about them. Open your heart and ask God to show you the gift in each and how He would like for you to respond. Your heart will soften, and so will your words.

Starting to find gratitude with the food on your plate is the easier part of the equation. The more difficult area to cultivate true thankfulness is what's in the mirror. I may not know what's it's like to walk this earth classified as overweight or obese. But I know what it's like to not like the skin you live in and desire for your outward appearance to change thinking it will improve your self-esteem.

ENJOY GOOD HEALTH

My twenties were the toughest decade of my life in terms of body dysmorphia and being swallowed up by the comparison typhoon of our culture. My entire self-worth was wrapped up in superficial numbers: weight, pants size, and pace per mile. I wore my extra small clothes as a badge of superiority. Keeping up with the rigid lifestyle to stay outwardly on point about drove me mad. Striving to stay skinny sucked the joy out of every corner of my life. I was miserable and sick on the inside.

Playing the comparison game is a good way to squash the joy right out of your life. All of us are susceptible to the trap of comparing our health and looks to others. Our culture is built on telling young girls and women that they are broken and that something is wrong with them in order to sell them something that will fix it.

The truth is that there will always be someone who looks better, runs faster, or eats cleaner than you. What I really need you to fully understand is that even if everyone on the planet ate and moved in the exact same way, we'd all still look completely different. And that is the way God wanted it. No two humans have the same fingerprints or exact same body shape. You are a one of a kind masterpiece and ultimately a temple for God to reside. When you bad mouth your body, you are basically telling God He does crappy carpentry work.

> *I praise you because I am fearfully and wonderfully made; your works are wonderful, I know that full well.—Psalm 139:14 (NIV)*

I spent years of precious mental and physical energy, time, and financial resources, pursuing a distorted version of an "ideal body" that had been planted and reinforced by social standards, not spiritual ones. It wasn't until I pondered how God might feel about me being so displeased with the body He gave me that I experienced true remorse for being so hard on my outward self.

Slowly, I started to realize that social standards are the problem, not my body. Knowing that God is the ultimate Creator, and for whatever reason, He gave me this body for His own purpose. I started reflecting on my intentions and thoughts behind feeling such strong urges to change it in terms of superficial achievements. I kindly remind myself of Psalm 139:14 whenever the newest diet product, trend, the program comes out, or I start to spiral into stinking thinking.

This isn't to say that if you act on caring for your body in a manner, you know to be spiritually sound and are well motivated that your outward appearance won't change. It also doesn't mean that enjoying a strong physique or pursuing athletic goals is un-Godly. The bottom line is, what are your motives, intentions, and what are you saying about your precious body ordained before the beginning of time by God to be yours? If your mind isn't calm and peaceful when you stand naked in the mirror, you might have some soul searching to do. As I said, this might be simple, but it isn't easy. You can move toward a healthier body inside and out, and still show loving-kindness to the body you live in today.

Explore: Cultivate the habit of showing self-love to the body you have today. Take time each day to speak out loud Psalm 139:14 into a mirror. Make a note or journal one positive thing about your body. Give thanks for legs that move, arms that hold your children, a belly that can laugh, or the ability to smell, hear, see, or feel the world around you. You can find one thing every day to thank the Lord for in terms of your physical vessel.

> *Your fasting ends in quarreling and strife, and in striking each other with wicked fists. You cannot fast as you do today and expect your voice to be heard on high*
> *—Isaiah 58:4 (NIV)*

In the first chapter, I touched on fasting and how there are spiritual rewards to fasting for the right reasons. Let's revisit the idea of fasting, but this time including what comes out of our mouth as much as what we put into it. Isaiah 58, teaches on what is considered to be "true fasting." It would serve you well to spend time reading the chapter in its entirety to grasp the message. The scene that you encounter is a dialogue between the Israelites and their God. They had been fasting and felt that God wasn't paying any attention. God points out they were fasting with wrong motives, and that they had behaviors in their lives that needed to be dealt with.

True fasting is meant to break down the flesh's grip on our behaviors. If the flesh is our puppeteer, it is then fasting that cuts the strings binding us to an unholy master. Traditional fast can include not eating or drinking certain foods, but that is not the purpose of this chapter. The Israelites of Isaiah 58, had been abstaining from food, but they had missed the real point. God told them they were fasting with wrong intentions; therefore, their request being made would not be acknowledged. It is easy to fast from something outside of ourselves. Anyone can abstain from bread, alcohol, chocolate or sodas for a specified number of days. Letting go on internal, almost automatic thoughts and feelings are on another level of fasting.

Isaiah 58 is full of wonderful and profound promises. You can't run around doing and saying your own thing and expect to get

ENJOY GOOD HEALTH

Godly blessings from it. Instead, find out what God wants for your health and seek and speak that. If you and I really want the blessing of God upon our health and life, we can't say whatever we want to say, whenever we want. We have to use our mouths to bless God, our bodies, and others. It would be a good idea to think of putting our mouth on a fast and see what blessings come from it.

May these words of my mouth and this meditation of my heart be pleasing in your sight, Lord, my Rock and my Redeemer--Psalm 19:14 (NIV)

Our prayer - *God, I realize I need your power to tame my tongue. Mine is not enough. I have struggled for years with stinking thinking and poor self-image, and relinquishing it will not be easy. Help me to trust you and to replace my pitiful self-talk with your powerful Word. Help me to let go of self-sabotaging self-talk and unleash the secret power of your Word I have held back from myself. Amen.*

Chapter 7
Control Emotional Eating

Feelings are much like waves, we can't stop them from coming, but we can choose which one to surf—Jonatan Martensson

Experts estimate that the average person has between 60,000-80,000 thoughts a day. That is an average of 2,500-3,300 per hour, and many of those thoughts trigger a corresponding emotion. A gamut of feelings is part of the human experience, and they can be very strong and demanding. Emotional eating is a leading cause of self-sabotaging a healthy living plan. It can feel as though your feelings rule your life and food choices. Regardless if you are sad, mad, frustrated, happy, celebratory, or just plain bored, it can seem that feelings can override your best-made health plan.

When you start thinking about what you are thinking about, you will start to realize that you talk about how you feel more than anything else. Tuning in to your feelings, you will quickly learn that emotions are ever-changing and can change without notification. Some days it can seem like your feelings have a mind of their own and do as they please for no specific reason. It can become fiercely frustrating to try and figure out why your mood can be so unstable. I haven't figured out how to control which feelings get triggered, but I have learned that talking about how I feel increases the intensity of those feelings. I also know that you don't have to wait to see how you feel every day before you know how you will act or what you choose to eat.

Yes, your daily emotions can be intense and trying, but you don't have to let them rule your life or food choices. It is going to take some work, but you can learn to manage your emotions rather than allowing them to manage you. Nothing is more empowering than feeling a wave of emotion rise from within that would have once sent you on a spiral of unwanted snack attacks and overruled it. You need to recognize God gave you free will, and you can make decisions that are not based on feelings. This Bible truth is key to consistently enjoying good health on a daily basis. Understand those feelings, like food is neither good nor evil. Emotions are unstable by nature and must be managed, not avoided, or stuffed. You and I have all the power needed to be good stewards of our emotions.

Explore: We all have emotions that trigger us more than others. If food is your coping method of choice, your list of feelings that trigger you may run the spectrum of unhappy to happy, and everything in between. Be honest with yourself and journal the feelings that trigger you to ditch your diet the most. Recall specific accounts of when your emotions got the best of you. Acknowledge any ongoing battle with certain emotions that end up with you eating or drinking unfavorable portions to cope.

Then you will know the truth, and the truth will set you free.—John 8:32 (NIV)

Before you can fully start to manage your emotions, you must learn the difference between how you feel and the reality of any given situation. Often our feelings are triggered by more than "what actually happened." The thing you can appreciate about facts is that they are true whether your flesh is willing to accept it or not. We are all emotional and sensitive people to some extent, but learning to search out the facts and not lean into feelings can empower you to change your life. Whether someone hurt your feelings, enraged you, or made you overjoyed, facts about the situation should be your true north on how to respond.

Emotions are at the core of our motivations. Being sensitive or emotional is not a bad thing. Experiencing feelings is part of the magic that is the human experience. However, feelings are often dictated by the flesh, and the trouble comes when we allow them to be stronger than the Holy Spirit's voice and prompting. How you feel each day about any given thing can be determined by past experiences, unrelated acute instances, and affected by what else is worrying you. Even how much sleep or caffeine you've had may influence your fickle feelings. It's not that you can't trust your feelings; you just need to investigate the facts, first.

When you find yourself being triggered and emotions rising up in you that makes you want to lash out, retreat, or go all-in, ask yourself what actually just happened. It may be true that a car cut you off, your children made you late, you spilled your coffee, or your boss added more work. The scale may have gone in the wrong direction. You may have lost a job, a loved one, or have a family member in despair. The list of potential emotional roller coasters are endless and always occurring. Searching for the facts means you are able to slow down, get real honest about the situation, and ask yourself what literally happened minus how it made you feel.

You may have gotten cut off, but did that person really wake up and decide to search you out and turn in front of you? When your children run late, ask yourself if there are ways to prepare the night better before or wake them up earlier to save time. Sometimes coffee gets spilled, or a waiter gets an order wrong. It doesn't mean your day is doomed. A stagnant scale or one that is moving in the wrong direction isn't out to ruin your life. With a little investigation, you could uncover logical explanations for it. Recognize that loss is part of life, and everyone goes through it at some point. While grief can be gut-wrenching, throwing your health out the window isn't going to bring anyone or thing back. The truth may not comfort you like a warm piece of the pie, but food won't fix your problems either.

Joyful emotions can also lead us astray when it comes to food and beverage decisions. Americans are hardwired to celebrate with comfort foods and decadent desserts. Holidays, birthdays, and anniversaries are annual events that don't seem complete without a feast, toast, or something sweet. Promotions, victories, and college football season also brings about platters of food and an expectation to wine and dine. While marking these occasions with extra flare is fun, and it can be argued that these limited dates are the perfect time to indulge, it can get out of hand quickly. You can celebrate the happiest of moments by soaking it all in and enjoying desserts or drinks responsibly.

Your feelings can be an indicator of red flags that need to be addressed. They can also be ridiculous overreactions that cause more unnecessary suffering. You can't decipher what is actually going on until you calm your mind and search for the facts. Following Psalm 46:10, you need to be still in order to know what is going on. Feelings will come rolling in like a tidal wave, and you must learn to ride the wave and refuse to make any major life or food decision until the sea on the inside has settled. This process isn't an easy one and will take lots of practice. But it is far less painful than living your life feeling like your world is crashing in on you every time a fleeting feeling arises from within.

Return to your list of trigger emotions you journaled that often land you on the other end of a food binge. In the beginning, it is going to seem like changing the response to those emotions is impossible. But that isn't because you are broken, you are just hardwired through years of conditioning to respond the way you do. The Bible doesn't offer insight into conditioning, but the science of psychology does. In the simplest terms, conditioning occurs when you learn to associate two different stimuli. The pavlovian theory is the famous experiment that Ivan Pavlov conducted with his dogs.

Pavlov discovered that dogs would get excited and salivate when food was placed in front of them. He wanted to see if he could condition the animals to associate food with additional stimuli. Upon feeding the dogs, as usual, Pavlov began ringing a bell along with mealtime. Soon after, the dogs began to associate the bell with food and would salivate upon hearing the bell without seeing the actual food. Not implying humans are dogs, but we are just as susceptible to becoming conditioned or trained as our furry friends. Marketing and advertising firms have been using these same principals to get us to associate certain brands or products with lifestyles, holidays, or happiness. You can use the same science for reconditioning your response to tricky triggers.

Everyone's self condition responses to stress, discouragement, or heightened feelings are different. Using the example of a hard day at work, you might come home and cope with eating cookies, pouring a glass of wine, or going through the drive-thru. It is how you have learned to let go and remove yourself from the situation and dive into something that brings you pleasure, even if it is for a short period of time. Over time, you become so conditioned that the moment your boss or client asks something extra from you, visions of how you will cope pop into your mind. Conditioning like everything else isn't good or bad. It is how the conditioning is affecting your overall health and happiness that matters. If you are an emotional eater learning to recondition your response will be a positive shift in your life.

Reconditioning can happen, but it will take time. Often you are unaware that there are years of repetitive responses that you are fighting against on a neurological level. That is why the first time you try a hot tea over a cold chardonnay and don't get the same relaxing effects you throw in the towel. Or, taking a fifteen-minute walk doesn't do the trick like a doughnut from the breakroom. The trick to reconditioning is trial and error and time. Finding a suitable new response for your trigger and giving yourself grace while enough time passes to create a new conditioned response. For you, reading a book may not do what climbing the stairs after a snarky email was sent. A hot bath may be better to relax than a hot cup of tea.

> *Thus the saying 'One sows and another reaps' is true. –*
> *John 4:37 (NIV)*

Throughout stories in the Bible, sowing is used as a metaphor for one's actions and reaping the results of those actions. Another way of saying it is if nothing changes, nothing changes. If you don't attempt to change your response to your triggers, the way you respond will never change. You must spend time sowing new seeds, new outcomes before you can start to reap new responses and, ultimately, healthier outcomes. Give yourself grace and accept that this will be a trial and error effort that will also take time.

Explore: Take your list of trigger emotions and start to brainstorm healthier responses. Give yourself three to five different approaches to try for each. And give yourself three to five weeks, giving it all you have before ditching a new response is useless. Keep journaling what works and what doesn't. You'll start to see a pattern of positive behaviors you can sow that will reap the responses you desire.

The intention of this chapter and the last is to help you connect the idea that the quality of your overall health will never rise higher than the quality of your internal thoughts and attitudes. There is a cycle at work that starts with a thought, which manifests into words, which creates your emotions, which determine your actions. Life is nothing more than a series of personal actions that produce consequences which you endure the fruits of daily. You have spent so much time focused on changing your behavior but overlooking the root of your actions: thoughts.

Thoughts → Words → Emotions → Actions

Once you start thinking about what you are thinking about, you will begin to notice that some stinking thoughts are fleeting. A wave of emotion rides through your veins like high tide and then quickly rolls away. Those thoughts could be the combination of a bad day, a disappointment, or PMS, to name a few. You know it is just a fleeting fury of the flesh when you can pull out a positive prayer card and feel somewhat better. You can pinpoint the trigger of your irrational emotion. Even on really emotional days, you usually wake up feeling more normal and go on the next day.

The more difficult thoughts to shake are the ones I don't want you to gloss over or make excuses to not deal with properly. The thoughts that are mocking what this book is trying to encourage you to do. An inner heckler that repeatedly is telling you that this may work for some, but it won't for you. Somehow you are a different kind of Christian, and this woo-woo stuff isn't going to help you. It is the deep-seated beliefs or assumed truths that seemed to be hardwired into your internal dialog like it's part of your DNA. No matter how hard you try to see the light on this wellness journey, you still are bombarded with discouragement, doubts, and fears.

Fear is one of the hardest feelings to learn to control. Fear can feel like quicksand, paralyzing you to move forward while simultaneously giving the sense of drowning at the moment. It can come on quickly and overtake you, or it can be an underlying sensation that is with you from daylight to dark. Fear can also be defined as panic, dread, distress, anxiety, worry, angst, unease, apprehension, nervousness, unrest, doubt, suspicion, or just being in a funk. All of these unpleasant emotions caused by the belief that someone or something is a threat is universal to us all. If your life's baseline emotion is some degree of fear, it becomes easy to see how eating fruits and vegetables, and getting in exercise may be the last thing on your mind.

In Mind Over Fork, I dedicated an entire chapter to defining fears that may be weighing you down. Deep-seated fears like the fear of intimacy for those who have been abused sexually, physically, verbally, or emotionally can manifest into an outward armor of weight that unconsciously puts a barrier between them and others. The fear of the unknown or FOMO, the fear of missing out, will keep the unhealthiest of people trapped in a destructive lifestyle. A person who grew up in a food-insecure home or had emotionally or physically absent parents or spouses may unconsciously fear the sensation of hunger. Hunger signifies lack, and for some people, that is too hard to handle, which leads to endless, mindless eating. Finally, it's worth pondering if you have a fear of actually succeeding at weight loss, or creating a healthy lifestyle. Without knowing it, you could fear that the fairytale of accomplishing your ideal body won't give you the life you associate with it.

> *Return to your fortress, you prisoners of hope; even now I announce that I will restore twice as much to you.—Zechariah 9:12 (NIV)*

Isaiah: 43:1 instructs, "Don't fear, for I have redeemed you; I have called you by name; you are Mine."God actually commands us not to fear or worry. The phrase "fear not" is used at least eighty times in the Bible, and many more with phrases like "do not be afraid." God realizes the enemy uses fear to decrease our joy, hope, and limit our victories. The antidote to fear is hope. Hope is a feeling of expectation and desire for positive things to happen. Believers can be a prisoner to fear or to hope. Often our "hope" is actually just us being cautiously optimistic while still doubting God. While you are on this new enlightened wellness journey, don't fall into the trap of downplaying what God can do to change your health and relationship with food and your self-image. Refuse to have one foot in fear and the other in hope as a defensive mechanism to not be too disappointed if it doesn't transpire as you wish.

In Zechariah 9:12, you are instructed to become a prisoner of hope and to receive a double portion of your prepared blessing when you go all-in with God. What kind of prisoner are you? One of doubts and unbelief just moving through the motions with a sour attitude not really expecting God's goodness? Or are you a prisoner of hope? Someone who refuses to stop believing like Abraham or Moses or Noah or Jesus or insert great — when all human reason for hope was gone, they hoped in faith and saw God's greatest promises come to pass. Y'all it does not do you any good to be hopeless. You can't revive God's unmerited favor without believing He's capable if you're in a dry season of receiving. Stay a prisoner of Hope! Don't let the world or any stinking thinking unshackle your chains of faith!

ENJOY GOOD HEALTH

If you find yourself shaking your head and feel like you have a persistent sad, anxious, or empty mood towards life, I will encourage you to find help beyond this book. Feelings of guilt, worthlessness, helplessness, and ongoing pessimism about your ability to take control of your health is a clear sign that you could benefit from talking with someone face to face. Take this as a catalyst to meet with a trusted pastor, women's minister, or faith-based counselor. There is no shame in reaching out for a wise council. This is not an area for a health coach, registered dietitian, or personal trainer. When the inner dialogue is so loud with negativity, you can't see a ray of hope; it's time to reach out for professional help.

> Keep this in mind: The devil wants you to pay attention to your feelings; Jesus wants you to pay attention to His truth.

Our prayer - *God, I confess today that I too often let my feelings take control of my food choices. Following Jesus with my whole heart and whole health is not about my feelings being in control but Him being in control. Teach me today that I can trust you and your promptings. Help me to discern between the facts and the feelings. Help me to control my feelings and not allow them to control me. Lead me in the obedient way. Amen.*

Chapter 8
Make Space for Good Health

Jesus said, "Come off by yourselves; let's take a break and get a little rest." For there was constant coming and going. They didn't even have time to eat—Mark 6:31 (MSG)

Americans aren't well. A study published by the Mayo Clinic showed that 70 percent of Americans take at least one prescription medication, and 20 percent are on five or more medications. People pop pills to cure more than just chronic diseases or lose weight. According to Medco Health Solutions, Inc. in 2010, more than one in five American adults take medicines for psychiatric disorders such as anxiety and depression. The Centers for Disease Control and Prevention (CDC) estimates 4 percent of adults use prescription medication to sleep. There seems to be a pill for every ill. And it appears Americans prefer to medicate and muster on rather than repair a hazardous lifestyle.

A quick internet search of the health effects of chronic stress and long term lack of sleep have similar consequences. Unmanaged stress can contribute to health problems such as high blood pressure, heart disease, obesity, and diabetes. Prolonged sleepless nights also affect your overall health and contribute to, you guessed it, obesity, heart disease, high blood pressure, and diabetes. It's easy to brush stress under the rug and drink an extra cup of coffee, thinking you are cheating death. But are you really? Heart disease is the leading cause of death for both men and women, and diabetes the 7th leading cause of death in the United States. When you tack on a load of stress and a loss of sleep to a poor diet and sedentary lifestyle, you become a ticking time bomb.

There isn't a single person who woke up this morning and jumped out of bed, ready to have a heart attack, stroke, or unmanaged blood sugar. No one gets giddy to get a life-threatening diagnosis from their doctor. That would be ludicrous. I haven't met anyone that wouldn't enjoy more sleep or less stress. You won't find a family on the planet that doesn't wish for good health and bountifulness of joy. It could be argued that a well-balanced life is a modern-day "promised land." In the Bible, the promised land was in contrast to the wilderness wanderings, and it was a land of plenty. Many of you have been in the wellness wilderness for far too long and seek plenty of rest.

Health experts unanimously agree that lifestyle factors such as diet and exercise are considered the most effective way to prevent and manage both heart disease and diabetes. Reducing stress and improving your quality of sleep both are dramatically improved by removing and revamping your basic lifestyle. Which, in turn, helps you prevent or manage your chronic disease. When given a choice, though, would you actually do it? Without pills, powders, or magical potions, it will require you going against the grain of the world's expectations of a productive, multitasking life.

Bullet point diet advice will not create the change you crave. Excuses to not exercise don't keep the chronic disease from knocking at your door. The hardest piece to the wellness puzzle is taking a hard look at your daily schedule and making space for good health. Good health is more than eating fruits and vegetables and getting in your mandatory minutes of physical activity.

Biblical good health includes mental, physical, and spiritual well-being. It's living a life that manages stress, provides quality sleep and includes a well-nourished body in motion. Making space for spiritual time, observing the Sabbath, and maintaining a schedule that allows you to breath is the hardest healthy habit to cultivate. However, out of all the other steps, simply adding more free time to your day can manifest indescribable healing powers capable of transforming your overall well-being.

People have embraced decluttering of material things: clothes, cabinets, and closets, to name a few. Sorting, organizing, and getting rid of items that no longer spark joy has become a cultural movement. However, when it comes to decluttering our calendars, it seems to be impossible. Simplifying our schedules, so we feel less rushed, stressed, and frazzled, appears to be a sign of weakness in our culture. Wearing the busy badge of honor has become the norm.

Our daily timelines have become crammed with worldly to-dos at the expense of our health and happiness. The unscheduled time that you can use in whatever way refreshes you or helps you get back on track feels more like a fantasy than a possibility. Everyone wants more time, but we all get 24 hours in a day. It's time to learn how to utilize them for your health's sake.

ENJOY GOOD HEALTH

So I hated life; because the work that is done under the sun was grievous to me. All of it is meaningless, a chasing after the wind. I hated all the things I had toiled for under the sun, because I must leave them to the one who comes after me.—Ecclesiastes 2:17-18 (NIV)

It sounds like Solomon was in a stressful phase of life and might have had a particularly hard day when he wrote the second chapter in Ecclesiastes. We've all had days where we felt like our work was useless and never-ending, finding no joy in our tasks. You have to read between the lines, but it would be fair to think that he may have been worn-out, stressed, and stretched too thin. Solomon was on a hamster wheel trying to maintain more worldly stuff. It broke him emotionally, and he snapped. At some point, he has an ah-ha moment that living by the world's standards was at the cost of his mental and spiritual health.

What do people get for all the toil and anxious striving with which they labor under the sun? All their days their work is grief and pain; even at night their minds do not rest. This too is meaningless.—Ecclesiastes 2:22-23 (NIV)

Solomon finally connected the dots. Being a workaholic or glamorizing productivity creates grief and pain. Ever feel like your mind is not able to rest at night? All the going and doing without taking time for rest and rejuvenation becomes meaningless and harmful to your health. Solomon realizes that a person can do nothing better than to eat and drink and find satisfaction in their own toil, and without God, you can not have enjoyment (vs. 24). If you are one of those overcommitted, more is better kind of people, I'd ask you, do you really enjoy that mindset? If not, what will it take to get you to realize less is more? Can we at least agree that operating as caffeine-filled zombies, isn't God's best for our life?

You don't have to be a workaholic to be out of balance and stressed out. Stay at home parents, and people pleasers of all kinds can volunteer their only nonrenewable resources away: time. Saying yes to every opportunity to serve the church, the school, or the community isn't helpful if you are running on fumes and failing to care for your health. One of the hardest lessons a people pleaser must learn is that "No" is a complete sentence. Just because you can squeeze something in doesn't mean you should do it. And just because someone thinks you would be perfect for the task, doesn't mean God is calling you to do it. Even Steve Jobs understood that deciding what not to do is as important as deciding what to do.

Overscheduling isn't just for adults. This isn't a book on parenting, but an idea to ponder is what message are we sending our kids by allowing their schedules to be hectic. Their mental and spiritual health matters, too. You may think you are sacrificing a few short years of sleep and sanity by spinning your minivan wheels taxing kids to the extreme, but you don't realize you are doing it at the cost of your health and your family's overall happiness. With grace, ask yourself, would you want your stressed and restless lifestyle for your children? Would you be happy to peer into the future and see your children grow into overworked, overscheduled, barely hanging on adults? It's our job to model a well-balanced life and give them the gift of a well-balanced family.

I'll admit that rest is a four-letter word, figuratively and literally. Making time for rest has been a difficult lesson for me to learn. I am one that wears the busyness badge of honor and gets satisfaction out of ticking off my to-do list. Bulldozing through my day only to lay in bed with mind wound up like an eight-day clock. For years I found it hard to breathe simply and struggled to keep up with the demands I had created for myself in my professional and personal life. I was too burnt out to even think about rest and stayed in survival mode. I was exhausted. I've been working for the last several years to change that. The most positive difference after making space in my calendar is in my relationships. My relationship with Jesus and myself has soared to new heights, positively influencing every area of my life. Fewer to-dos mean more time to listen, engage, and be present with the things my heart knows matters most.

Explore: When you hear the word rest, what comes to mind? If you're honest, even though the idea of rest is supposed to be refreshing and inviting, our work-based culture has turned resting into a foreign concept. Even the thought of unstructured free time can stress us out. Many Christians know that keeping the Sabbath is one of the Ten Commandments, but think going to church for an hour on Sunday is a get-out-of-jail-free card and move about a busy checklist. Balanced living is blasphemy by the world's standards, but it's Biblical at the core. The good news is that Jesus' response to our lack of rest isn't condemning but an open invitation to retreat and reconnect.

ENJOY GOOD HEALTH

"Come to me, all you who are weary and burdened, and I will give you rest.—Matthew 11:28 (NIV)

The foundation of this book is to encourage you to enjoy good health, but quite frankly, you can't do that without learning to rest, too. It's easy to forget that Jesus understands our humanity. While Jesus was on earth, He experienced exhaustion and work fatigue. Weariness, anxiety, and stress were all emotions that Jesus can relate to experiencing. In Mark 4: 35-40, Jesus recognizes that there is plenty of work to be done. When you turn your Bible there, you will read of a scene filled with a crowd. People who have traveled far and wide, looking for healing and teaching. Even with so much outside expectation looming, Jesus tells His disciples to get in the boat. Once in the boat, Jesus naps! Jesus understood He couldn't give the people crying for his talents the full breadth of who He was without stopping to rest.

Even with all the important things Jesus had to do, He made space in the midst of a chaotic world to rest. If He needed space in His daily schedule to be effective, you and I most certainly do, too. Jesus also encouraged his disciples to rest, regardless of the workload and expectations that were required of them. Jesus was aware of the constant coming and going of the disciples' schedules, to the point they didn't even have time to sit and eat a meal. As a well-balanced leader should, He encouraged them to get away from the needy crowds, the task, and the mission for a break and get a little rest. (Mark 6:31) Needy crowds include, but are not limited to your family, church, work, and social circles.

Rest can sound inactive and unproductive, but that is the

furthest thing from the truth. Rest is one of only three objectives named in the New Testament. Preach the Gospel (Romans 15:20) and please God (2 Corinthians 5:9) are the other two ambitions. As I get older with more experience adding rest into the fabric of my day, I am starting to understand that you can't adequately serve God or keep His commands without a clear, well-rested body and mind. Emotionally speaking, humans are at their worst when they are tired. I am my least favorite version of myself as a spouse, parent, co-worker and disciple when I lack sleep and rest. My mouth is harder to control when my body is fatigued, and I find myself apologizing for allowing my feelings to get the best of me.

Rest, even in small spaces in the day, allowing you to slow down and pause. This is a way to put God in His rightful place. To rest means to cease from labor. The world loves to label us by what we do, our potential to perform. When you take time to breathe and be silent or still, you are signaling to God and the world that you are not on the throne. Your works are not your identity, and your productivity is not a punch card to more salvation. Small moments of surrender throughout the day brings you back to the center. Imagine what a typical weekday would be like if you gave yourself permission to let go of the expectations you and others push you to be or do.

> *"Remember the Sabbath day by keeping it holy. Six days you shall labor and do all your work, but the seventh day is a Sabbath to the Lord your God. On it you shall not do any work, neither you, nor your son or daughter, nor your male or female servant, nor your animals, nor any foreigner residing in your towns. For in*

six days the Lord made the heavens and the earth, the sea, and all that is in them, but he rested on the seventh day. Therefore the Lord blessed the Sabbath day and made it holy.—Exodus 20:8-11 (NIV)

How Christians are to observe the Sabbath is a hot topic of debate. As a dietitian, not a theologian, I'm not here to imply which day of the week is the best day for the Sabbath or how you should spend it. But it wouldn't be right to write a chapter on rest and not mention the fact that observing the Sabbath is so important to God; it is part of the big Ten Commandments. In Genesis, you find that God rested on the seventh day from all His work, and then He blessed that day. In Exodus, you find more detail in what believers should do on that day: nothing much. Taking a full 24-hours to stop our work and rest alines us with God's Holy rhythm for life. Work hard, rest up, and repeat.

Trust me. I am a work in progress when it comes to unplugging and unwinding for a full day. It is an area I am striving to improve, but I can't deny that it is an essential piece of enjoying good health. Taking any steps to observe the Sabbath better as it is desired in scripture will reap the peaceful rewards in your life. Our human brain, our bodies, our spirits, and our emotions reboot when we disconnect with the demands of our worldly life and enjoy the best parts of the human experience: faith, family, and freedom from the to-do list. Isaiah 14:7 sums it up; the whole earth is at rest and is quiet; they break forth into shouts of joy. Relax in silence and bring forth the joy.

Explore: Take out your calendar and write down all your responsibilities and obligations from work to carpool, to spin class, to grocery trips, and any task in between. Especially make a note of those tasks that repeat weekly. Add to the list your children's activities that you are responsible for transportation, church meetings, date nights, volunteer gigs, and any other duty that takes up your time and demands your presence. Get it all out on paper. Go down the list and circle the task only you can do. Typically, that is work and family-related. Underline all tasks that spark joy at the thought of completing it. For me, that would include church, fitness, and volunteering with organizations I believe in. Cross out any task that brings forth an eye roll or the realization someone else could do it, and you would never be missed. Take this list to your prayer time and start to ask for help saying "No" to task with a big x on it.

Making space for good health means you have a built-in "emergency fund" into your day for when you're running late or a child throws up, or a friend needs your attention. Margin is your moment to sip a cup of tea and enjoy arriving at a meeting a few minutes early. It's your opportunity to breath and simply move through your day. You can start by setting your margins and then filling in your to-dos or set your schedule but put distinguished buffers between tasks. If you travel between obligations, double your travel time, and that will provide a safe buffer zone.

Weekly ask yourself, what gives you room to breathe, and what do you need to do to feel less frazzled? A margin in the morning would provide you, what? It could be enjoying your coffee on the back porch, doing a devotional, getting to work on time, etc. A margin in the evenings could provide you time to read a book, cook a meal, or get in a half-hour of physical activity. Your weekends need margins, too. Saturday and Sunday should be spent with the Sabbath in mind. Make time to have the opportunity to take a walk, be spontaneous, or do like Jesus and take a nap!

Once you decide where you want your margins to be, guard them. Commit and refuse to plan anything into your schedule that would override those boundaries. Make your margin time as important as a task with consequences. Start to protect date night with your spouse, going to Bible study, volunteering in ministry, or biking the neighborhood with your children. In the beginning, you are going to feel like you're wasting precious time doing frivolous things. Fight that urge and begin to retrain your brain to think about what gives you margin. Remind yourself it is Godly to rest and recharge.

How to add in free-time is up to you, but skimming over this chapter as a fantasy is not acceptable. I have found that keeping your life well-balanced is a constant effort. You will always be balancing out and weighing your obligations as long as you're active in society. This isn't to discourage you, but to inform you that there is no perfect scheduling method to balance. Every day, you will wake up, pray, and move through your day intentionally, making the best decisions with your time, with Jesus in mind. Say, No in the name of Jesus, to things that don't serve you, your health, or family well. And when there is constant coming and going, imagine Jesus telling you to get off by yourself and take a break and get a little rest.

Our prayer - *Lord, I know my time belongs to you. Every minute of every day you give me is precious. Help me use the time wisely, investing in my health and things that matter.*

ENJOY GOOD HEALTH

Make known idol tasks and give me strength to remove them. Show me where to expand my margin time to provide a peaceful pace and not hurried one. May I learn to rest in your presence and recharge my connection to the Holy Spirit. Amen.

Chapter 9
The cost of Western "Wellness"

A thief is only there to steal and kill and destroy. I came so they can have real and eternal life, more and better life than they ever dreamed of—John 10:10 (MSG)

There is an unseen battle going on as we go about our lives. We don't see it, and can't fully understand it. The Bible tells us our struggle is not against flesh and blood, but against the rulers, against the authorities, against the powers of this dark world and against the spiritual forces of evil in the heavenly realms. (Ephesians 6:12 NIV) In other dimensions, there is a spiritual war between good and evil, between God and Satan, between angels and demons.

As a child of God, the evil forces hate you. That puts you right in the middle of this unseen war. That is why the devil is out to be a thief, roaming the earth looking to steal and kill and destroy. To steal is defined to take without the intention to return it. I believe one of the biggest heists Satan has succeeded at in the West is robbing us of our attention and averting it to a fixation on the vanity in the form of wellness. The Western world has become engulfed in a preoccupation with youth and beauty, which steals our time, distracts us, and takes an uncanny amount of our money. Not to mention, evil drains our self-confidence and impedes our ability to love ourselves as God created fully.

ENJOY GOOD HEALTH

The wellness industry includes nutrition, fitness, and beauty products that offer claims to prompt health, retain youth, and change your outward appearance to become more attractive by the world's standards. The Global Wellness Institute (GWI) publishes the Global Wellness Economy Monitor, last released in October 2018, with data for 2017, and can be found in detail online. In 2017, GWI reported the global wellness industry was a $4.2 trillion market. The industry is continuing to grow, showing a 6.4 percent boost from 2015-2017. Of that personal care, beauty and anti-aging account for $1,083 billion, healthy eating, nutrition, and weight loss for $702 billion, and fitness and mind-body comes in at $595 billion. It is mind-boggling the money that is being poured into snake oil products with deceptive marketing and cure-all elixirs for creating well-being worldwide.

Comprehending $4.2 trillion dollars is hard. To illustrate, the height of a stack of 1,000,000,000,000 (trillion) one dollar bills measures approximately 67,866 miles. One trillion one-dollar bills would reach more than one-fourth of the way from the earth to the moon. The $4.2 trillion dollars worldwide wellness industry would reach beyond the moon! Think of it this way. If you were given a shopping spree and could spend $20 per second with a 1 trillion dollar limit, you could shop for 1,585 years without ceasing. Now, multiply that times 4.2 to get the full impact.

Explore: Think about all the money you have spent on wellness, not related to medications or treatment to actual health care. Supplements, vitamins, teas, powders, or patches bought in a wellness store or from a pyramid business: magazine subscriptions, gym fees, weight loss books, or any as-seen-on-TV products. Add to the brainstorm the amount of time you may spend in a day thinking about what you are going to eat, counting calories, reading articles on fad diets, or into the next weight loss product. Be honest and jot down true estimates of both time and money spent.

While $4.2 trillion is an unfathomable number for a global market, $155 per month hits home here in the United States. In a survey conducted by Myprotein covering 1,350 Americans aged 18 to 65, the results show how much each state spends on their health and fitness habits. The average American adult spends $155 per month on health and fitness. Add that up over 60 years, and it equals $112,000 on wellness in a lifetime. Within their survey, they found the average American spending $56 each month on supplementation. In fact, over 60 percent of the population spends more than $40 each month on nutritional supplements.

Money can be redirected or regained over time, but one thing that cannot be recouped once lost is time. In 2012, a group of UK researchers found that the average woman diets twice a year, losing her body weight over nine times during her life. The most surprising finding was women spend an alarming 17 years of their life on a diet. Researchers found that less than one percent of participants were able to stick to a diet for a 12 month period. A third of all women reported dieting for at least six months per year. Furthermore, more than one in three women shared they would splurge on comfort purchases like shoes when they felt bad about their weight. You could add those purchases to the total

ENJOY GOOD HEALTH

pocketbook impact of the diet culture, too.

How you spend your hard-earned cash is up to you. I'm not here to make you feel guilty about your purchases or the number of times you have been on a diet. Rather, I hope to challenge you to see how much of your mental and physical resources are going to a bottomless pit called a wellness industry. My prayer is that you see the bigger scheme that is at work and not is condemned but convicted to the scam. Corporations are lining their pockets with your insecurities while there are people around the world literally dying from things the West takes for granted. The West has some of the most educated and well-abled people capable of changing the world. But the devil keeps us distracted and preoccupied on the hamster wheel of wellness for up to 17 years! As long as we are obsessed with ourselves, we are less likely to open our eyes to those hurting from the issues we have the abilities and resources to help solve.

I mentioned earlier in this book that the devil doesn't care about your thighs, outward appearance, or health in general. But, he cares because you care. Roaming around looking for a slither of an opportunity to come in and steal your time, energy, and resources away from things that actually matter to God's Kingdom. Even if you don't feel led to saving the world, think of how you could better serve your family or community with an extra 17 years of focused mental energy? What would your finances look like if you made an extra $112,000 dollars over a lifetime, not thrown away on fickle products and quick fixes?

Investing in your health is a Biblical thing. Paying for a

gym membership, and actually using it is productive. Spending extra on fresh produce, supporting your farmer's markets, or taking a cooking class to better prepare heart-healthy dishes is money well spent. Taking up yoga or hiring a personal trainer to learn skills that will help you destress and build a strong body isn't inappropriate. Creating a bedroom conducive to better sleep is smart. Don't allow the message in this chapter to get twisted and accuse all money or energy spent on good health as the devil's diversion tactic. You're smart enough to know the difference between an impulse buy for a fat blaster off late-night TV versus a pair of running shoes to run your first 5K. Purchasing fresh produce is not the same as having a cabinet full of supplements with unrealistic claims. It all comes back to your motivation and intentions. Check your motives before checking out at the register.

> *And if you spend yourselves in behalf of the hungry and satisfy the needs of the oppressed, then your light will rise in the darkness, and your night will become like the noonday.—Isaiah 58:10 (NIV)*

For a moment, ponder with me what you could do in terms of Godly service, with half of the money spent on frivolous wellness purchases or mental energy lost on contemplating calories or fad diets. There are countless organizations and ways to serve the Kingdom. As a registered dietitian, my passion and knowledge of reputable organizations lie in those helping to end hunger. For that reason, let's look at the hypothetical impact $155 a month could have on feeding the hungry and satisfying the needs of the oppressed.

ENJOY GOOD HEALTH

In a nation that is battling obesity, it's hard to fathom that anyone in America goes hungry. Sadly, every day, there are millions of children and adults who do not get the meals they need to be in good health and thrive. Feeding America is a United States-based nonprofit organization that is a nationwide network of more than 200 food banks that feed more than 46 million people through food pantries, soup kitchens, shelters, and other community-based agencies. It is the third-largest U.S. charity and works with farmers, manufacturers, and retailers to get food to our neighbors in need.

Once you understand many of your neighbors in your community are forced to make tough choices between buying food and medical bills, food and housing, or food and transportation, you can start to feel convicted about taking groceries for granted. Stories of food insecurity from my home state of Mississippi, which has the highest percentage of hungry residents in the country, has moved me to tears and to action. You must realize that the struggle of hunger goes beyond harming an individual family's future, but it can harm us all. Food for every person is one critical piece to the puzzle to ensure all households have an active, healthy life.

Whether you believe it or not, you can help end hunger. Did you know that every ten dollars donation to Feeding America or one of their 200 food banks, like the Mississippi Food Network, provides sixty meals for our hungry neighbors? A monthly gift as small as ten dollars creates a reliable source of funding year-round to help provide meals and social services to families facing hunger, giving them a chance to thrive. The average American who spends $155 a month on wellness, in theory, could secure about 1000 meals a month to children and families. Multiply that 1000 meals times all the Americans who fall into that category and talk about making a wellness impact.

Plenty of domestic organizations fight hunger and malnutrition overseas. Millions are truly starving in underdeveloped countries. But God Ministries (BGM) is a non-profit organization that shares the love of Jesus Christ through building sustainable communities around the world. Part of BGM is the Pen Lavi (The Bread of Life) Malnutrition Center in Ganthier, Haiti, about 18 miles east of Port au Prince. There, children with acute malnutrition who have reached a point that they need very specialized daily care to heal and get quality care. Before Pen Lavi opened, malnourished patients had to figure out travel two hours away and often didn't receive nutrition education or counseling. A mere $155 monthly donation could sponsor a crib and pay for medicines, formulas, therapeutic foods, and more. Only $75 a month provides a mom a bed who is able to participate in their child's care and receive food, medical care when necessary, a Bible, and hygiene supplies. A simple $20 provides transportation to assist parents in getting to and from the clinic to work or care for other family members.

> Dear children, let us not love with words or speech
> but with actions and in truth.—1 John 3:18 (NIV)

Financial support isn't the only way to redirect what the West's obsession with wellness is stealing from the Kingdom. Your time can change lives and expand God's message and mission. According to researchers, women are spending 17 years of their life on a diet or dieting an average of 6 months out of every year. Imagine if collectively, we all spent half our year volunteering for things that truly make a difference. Volunteering doesn't have to take over your life or even half the year to be beneficial. In fact, research shows two to three hours per week of volunteering can help others and make you feel happier and be healthier.

Volunteering should feel like a fun and rewarding hobby, not another chore on your to-do list. With busy lives, it can feel impossible to find time to volunteer. You may need to purge your calendar to make room for volunteering. Before you start to make excuses to avoid spending time doing unpaid work, learn what the Bible says about volunteering. The Bible repeatedly praises the noble nature of helping those in need, which is the essence of volunteering. According to scripture, we are to love with our actions. Volunteering time to worthwhile causes is on the way to put Christianity in action. Not to mention, the right volunteering match can help you find friends, connect with your community, learn new skills, and even improve your health.

Giving your time to others has been shown to protect your mental and physical health. Did you know, volunteering can reduce stress, combat depression, stimulate you mentally, and provide a higher sense of purpose. Finding two to three hours a week to take your mind off your needs and addressing the needs of others provides healing for you and others that can't come from a pharmacy. Giving time in even the simplest ways can create a richer and more enjoyable life.

ENJOY GOOD HEALTH

Each of you should use whatever gift you have received to serve others, as faithful stewards of God's grace in its various forms.—1 Peter 4:10 (NIV)

Explore: Take time to identify your life's interests or professional gifts and connect them with ways to volunteer. What would you enjoy doing? The opportunities that match your interests are most likely to be fun and fulfilling. For example, ask yourself what you would do to improve your neighborhood, to pass on your passions to others, or what struggle would you enjoy seeing eliminated.

Places of worship are not the only place to spend your time helping others. You can look to libraries or senior centers for opportunities. Contact your service organizations such as Lions Clubs or Rotary Clubs for service projects. Youth organizations, sports teams, and after-school programs always need an extra helping hand. Historical restorations, national parks, and conservation organizations have fulfilling opportunities to serve, too. Even your community theaters, museums, and monuments can provide opportunities to share God's message. Don't limit God's ability to use your willingness to volunteer to only faith-based projects.

For we are God's handiwork, created in Christ Jesus to do good works, which God prepared in advance for us to do.—Ephesians 2:10 (NIV)

It doesn't take a significant financial or time commitment to make a substantial impact here or abroad. Together, our focused and committed contributions make a real difference in the health and lives of our neighbors and fellow humans who struggle. When Christians open their eyes and move past our own superficial lives here in the West, we can change the world. Again, it's not about condemning you for any purchase or wellness interest. I'm trying to challenge your thinking and expand the idea of well-being to all beings. How much of your financial and time investment in wellness is in vain, and how much could you divert to doing God's work?

The Devil can't steal what we protect against him. God prepared each of us with unique gifts and talents to do good works, not just to look good. In case you need to be reminded, you were not created to spend 17 years only to lose weight or have firm thighs. Turning our attention from the mirror to what truly matters to God is a first step in reclaiming and realigning the West's potential to be a powerhouse for the eternal Kingdom.

Our prayer - *God, thank you for helping to change my heart and my mind about what it means to be in good health. Relax my grasp on striving for the world's standards of beauty and health and help me to do my part in improving the health of others. Focus my attention on their needs and interests. Empower me to be your hands and feet as I look away from the mirror and turn my energy to nourishing your kingdom.*

Letter from the Author

Dear Friend,

You've come to the end of this book, but the beginning of a more profound well-being journey, if you choose it. Reading this book won't fix your problems with food or self-image. Exploring the scripture and spending time in silence, contemplating the more significant ideas with your Savior will have a profound effect on your health and life. It may take several trips back through the exploration exercises before it starts to click. Even after you experience some freedom from anxious thoughts and feelings that have lived rent-free in your head for years, you will have to continue to cultivate and renew your mind to stay the course.

You and I are on the same journey. Both of us, along with everyone else, want a balanced and healthy relationship with food and who we see in the mirror. But, understand, we're all on a different path. Our visions of what good health looks like will all differ. You picked up this book because, to some degree, your relationship with wellness needs repair. Continue to ask yourself what you hope to accomplish and keep that vision in front of you. More than anything, this book attempts to teach you a new language. Changing the way you talk about food, your health, and your ability to live well is the foundation for elevating your health. This new language includes affirming the body you have today, giving thanks for any food you choose, viewing a healthy lifestyle as a form of worship, and offering yourself grace along the way.

The world would like you to focus on what you have to sacrifice or give up to gain better health. No one understands sacrifice better than Jesus Christ. Anyone familiar with the Bible understands His sacrificial death at Calvary to atone for our sins. Christ crucifixion was indeed the greatest act of sacrifice the world has ever witnessed. And yet, He did it from a place of gratitude and joy.

ENJOY GOOD HEALTH

Parents find joy in sacrificing their time and resources to watch their children stay safe, grow, and experience life. To someone who doesn't have children, it can seem as though the sacrifices are painful and costly, but parents wouldn't trade those years of sacrifice for anything. Those who live in true health feel the same way about pouring time and energy into a balanced diet, physical activity, and managing stress. It's a privilege they don't take for granted.

The world would like you to feel entitled to instant gratification. Remember, very rarely are instant miracles found in the Bible. Miracles don't mature you. The day you plant the seed is not the day you eat the fruit. Be patient on your journey to balanced well-being. Be humble and seek help with uncontrollable emotions or anxious thoughts. Be willing to learn to cook healthier foods. Be relentless in managing your busy schedule and decreasing stress. Keep moving forward and know that all this hard work you're putting in, including fighting back the negativity in your mind, will produce healing results. Your time is now. Don't give up on your harvest before the rain comes.

Enjoying good health is an ongoing process. I've been fighting for the freedom to live healthy and balanced for years. I'm still learning and evolving as a dietitian and human being. I, too, have to eat and live in the body God designed for me. While I don't have all the answers for you, I know a few things to be true. Good health is not all or nothing, it's not black or white, and it's not right or wrong. Wellness is particular to the individual, and even then, that's subject to change. Nutrition is just the food and nourishment you consume. It doesn't have the credentials to fix any feeling or right any wrong you experience. You wouldn't intentionally crash your car on the way to work if you took a wrong turn. Don't wreck your wellness efforts because of a hard day or powerful temptation. Counting your blessings is more productive than counting calories. Lastly, God didn't put one person on this planet to spend their life losing weight. You and I have a more powerful purpose.

Explore: Your last assignment is to dive into the Bible and read about all the women who exceeded expectations. Start by getting to know the stories around Mary, Eve, Sarah, Miriam, Esther, Ruth, Naomi, Deborah, and Mary Magdalene. While your heart will be filled by what the Bible says about them, I want you also to be encouraged by what the writers never mentioned: their weight.

Do you not know that your bodies are temples of the Holy Spirit, who is in you, whom you have received from God? You are not your own; you were bought at a price. Therefore honor God with your bodies. 1 Corinthians 6:19-20 (NIV) Take care of your whole self. Permit yourself to let go of the world's standards of health. Weep when you need to weep. Rest when you need to rest. Eat with intention and move with purpose. With all my heart, I want you to go forth with grit and grace to live and eat with Jesus in mind.

Enjoy Good Health,
Rebecca Turner

Appendix

Healthy Vision Worksheet

Step1. Brainstorm words, ideas, phrases, terminology (etc.) that identifies **healthy** to you.

Step 2. Brainstorm all your **non-negotiables**. List foods, beverages, or habits that if you avoided for a decade or more would steal joy from your life.

Step 3. Eliminate all entries with tainted motivation. *This will take time in prayer and meditation. Ask God to reveal what is achievable, ideal, and right for this season of life.*

Step 4. Write down every diet, eating style, or fad you've tried to control your weight.

Step 5. List out the pros and cons for each entry in step 4.

Step 6. Assess your pros and cons for common threads and recurring themes that work or do not work for you and your lifestyle.

Step 7. Develop 3-5 SMART goals. (S- specific. M- measurable. A- achievable. R-relevant. T- Time-bound).

Step 8. Create 3-5 wellness worship cards filled with verses, psalms, or Biblical thoughts that will keep you motivated and encouraged.

Step 9. View SMART goals and wellness worship cards, daily.

Step 10. Reassess as needed, and never give up the fight for your God given right to enjoy good health!

About the Author

Author, registered dietitian nutritionist (RDN), radio host, television presenter, and a certified specialist in sports dietetics (CSSD) with the Academy of Nutrition and Dietetics.

Rebecca Turner has extensive broadcast and print media experience; specializing in creating multimedia content on diet and nutrition for the general public and competitive athletes.

Through print, TV, and radio, Rebecca Turner strives to provide sensible nutrition advice to a statewide and national audience. She lends her talents to Mississippi Public Broadcasting's healthy eating show, Fit to Eat, and the Emmy Award-winning children's show, Ed Said. Regularly, she appears on WLBT / FOX 40-TV as a wellness expert and creates nutrition-based features for national publications like *LifeWay HomeLife Magazine* and *Open Windows Devotionals*.

Rebecca Turner zealously spreads the message of her published book, Mind Over Fork, which offers a holistic approach to health and wellness, focused on nutritional advice, mindfulness, and behavior modification. At her home church, First Baptist Church of Brandon, and through social media, she combines her practical nutrition tips with her Christian faith to help women develop a healthy vision for their life based on God's Word, not the world's standards. Weekdays, you will find her hosting Good Things with Rebecca Turner, a statewide talk radio show on SuperTalk Mississippi.

Rebecca Turner graduated from the University of Southern Mississippi with both a bachelor and master of science degree in nutrition and food systems. In 2012, she was awarded the Mississippi Recognized Young Dietitian of the Year and received the Circle of Excellence Award from SUDIA in 2014.

www.ingramcontent.com/pod-product-compliance
Lightning Source LLC
Chambersburg PA
CBHW070948080526
44587CB00015B/2232